Fix-It and Forget-It®
SOUPS & STEWS

Nourishing Soups, Stews, Broths, Chilis & Chowders

127
Instant Pot®
& Slow Cooker
Recipes

T0049463

HOPE COMERFORD

Photos by Bonnie Matthews

Good Books

New York, New York

Copyright © 2023 by Good Books
Photos by Bonnie Matthews

Good Books books may be purchased in bulk at special discounts for sales promotion, corporate gifts, fund-raising, or educational purposes. Special editions can also be created to specifications. For details, contact the Special Sales Department, Good Books, 307 West 36th Street, 11th Floor, New York, NY 10018 or info@skyhorsepublishing.com.

Good Books is an imprint of Skyhorse Publishing, Inc.®, a Delaware corporation.

Visit our website at www.goodbooks.com.

10 9 8 7 6 5 4 3 2 1

Library of Congress Cataloging-in-Publication Data
Names: Comerford, Hope, author. | Matthews, Bonnie, photographer.
Title: Fix-it and forget-it soups & stews : nourishing soups, stews, broths, chilis & chowders : 127 Instant Pot & slow cooker recipes / Hope Comerford ; photos by Bonnie Matthews.
Description: New York, New York : Good Books, [2023] | Series: Fix-it and forget-it | Includes index. | Summary: "127 nourishing soups, stews, broths, chowders, and chilis"—Provided by publisher.
Identifiers: LCCN 2023015441 (print) | LCCN 2023015442 (ebook) | ISBN 9781680998962 (paperback) | ISBN 9781680999020 (epub)
Subjects: LCSH: Soups. | Stews. | Smart cookers. | Electric cooking, Slow. | LCGFT: Cookbooks.
Classification: LCC TX757 .C63 2023 (print) | LCC TX757 (ebook) | DDC 641.81/3—dc23/eng/20230403
LC record available at https://lccn.loc.gov/2023015441
LC ebook record available at https://lccn.loc.gov/2023015442

Cover design by David Ter-Avanesyan
Cover photo by Bonnie Matthews

Print ISBN: 978-1-68099-896-2
Ebook ISBN: 978-1-68099-902-0

Printed in China

Contents

Welcome to Fix-It and Forget-It Soups & Stews

Some of the best soups, stews, chowders, chilis, and broths can be made right from your slow cookers and Instant Pots! Your slow cooker allows you to add the ingredients and lets them simmer all day. Your Instant Pot allows you to develop amazing flavors in a much shorter amount of time than letting it simmer on the stove for hours.

With over 100 recipes, you are sure to find many future favorites. Don't know where to begin? I always suggest reading the book cover to cover. Learn some new things about your slow cooker and Instant Pot by reading the first few sections. Make some notes in the margin. Put together a grocery list. Then, pick a recipe and give it a go, knowing you're making a recipe that is tried and true!

Now, go grab the appliance of your choice, and cook with confidence! Your new favorite soups and stews await!

Choosing a Slow Cooker

Not all slow cookers are created equal . . . or work equally as well for everyone!

Those of us who use slow cookers frequently know we have our own preferences when it comes to which slow cooker we choose to use. For instance, I love my programmable slow cooker, but there are many programmable slow cookers I've tried that I've strongly disliked. Why? Because some go by increments of 15 or 30 minutes and some go by 4, 6, 8, or 10 hours. I dislike those restrictions, but I have family and friends who don't mind them at all! I am also pretty brand loyal when it comes to my manual slow cookers because I've had great success with those and have had unsuccessful moments with slow cookers of other brands. So, which slow cooker(s) is/are best for your household?

It really depends on how many people you're feeding and if you're gone for long periods of time. Here are my recommendations:

For 2–3 person household	3–5 quart slow cooker
For 4–5 person household	5–6 quart slow cooker
For a 6+ person household	6½–7 quart slow cooker

Large slow cooker advantages/disadvantages:

Advantages:
- You can fit a loaf pan or a baking dish into a 6- or 7-quart, depending on the shape of your cooker. That allows you to make bread or cakes, or even smaller quantities of main dishes. (Take your favorite baking dish and loaf pan along when you shop for a cooker to make sure they'll fit inside.)
- You can feed large groups of people, or make larger quantities of food, allowing for leftovers, or meals, to freeze.

Disadvantages:
- They take up more storage room.
- They don't fit as neatly into a dishwasher.
- If your crock isn't ⅔–¾ full, you may burn your food.

Small slow cooker advantages/disadvantages:

Advantages:
- They're great for lots of appetizers, for serving hot drinks, for baking cakes straight in the crock, and for dorm rooms or apartments.
- Great option for making recipes of smaller quantities.

Disadvantages:
- Food in smaller quantities tends to cook more quickly than larger amounts. So keep an eye on it.
- Chances are, you won't have many leftovers. So, if you like to have leftovers, a smaller slow cooker may not be a good option for you.

My recommendation:

Have at least two slow cookers; one around 3 to 4 quarts and one 6 quarts or larger. A third would be a huge bonus (and a great advantage to your cooking repertoire!). The advantage of having at least a couple is you can make a larger variety of recipes. Also, you can make at least two or three dishes at once for a whole meal.

Manual vs. Programmable

If you are gone for only six to eight hours a day, a manual slow cooker might be just fine for you. If you are gone for more than eight hours during the day, I would highly recommend purchasing a programmable slow cooker that will switch to warm when the cook time you set is up. It will allow you to cook a wider variety of recipes.

The two I use most frequently are my 4-quart manual slow cooker and my 6½-quart programmable slow cooker. I like that I can make smaller portions in my 4-quart slow cooker on days I don't need or want leftovers, but I also love how my 6½-quart slow cooker can accommodate whole chickens, turkey breasts, hams, or big batches of soups. I use them both often.

Get to Know Your Slow Cooker

Plan a little time to get acquainted with your slow cooker. Each slow cooker has its own personality—just like your oven (and your car). Plus, many new slow cookers cook hotter and faster than earlier models. I think that with all of the concern for food safety, the slow cooker manufacturers have amped up their settings so that "High," "Low," and "Warm" are all higher temperatures than in the older models. That means they cook hotter—and therefore, faster—than the first slow cookers. The beauty of these little machines is that they're supposed to cook low and slow. We count on that when we flip the switch in the morning before we leave the house for ten hours or so. So, because none of us knows what kind of temperament our slow cooker has until we try it out, nor how hot it cooks—don't assume anything. Save yourself a disappointment and make the first recipe in your new slow cooker on a day when you're at home. Cook it for the shortest amount of time the recipe calls for. Then, check the food to see if it's done. Or if you start smelling food that seems to be finished, turn off the cooker and rescue your food.

Also, all slow cookers seem to have a "hot spot," which is of great importance to know, especially when baking with your slow cooker. This spot may tend to burn food in that area if you're not careful. If you're baking directly in your slow cooker, I recommend covering the "hot spot" with some foil.

Take notes . . .

Don't be afraid to make notes in your cookbook. It's yours! Chances are, it will eventually get passed down to someone in your family and they will love and appreciate all of your musings. Take note of which slow cooker you used and exactly how long it took to cook the recipe. The next time you make it, you won't need to try to remember. Apply what you learned to the next recipes you make in your cooker. If another recipe says it needs to cook 7–9 hours, and you've discovered your slow cooker cooks on the faster side, cook that recipe for 6–6½ hours and then check it. You can always cook a recipe longer—but you can't reverse things if it's overdone.

Get creative . . .

If you know your morning is going to be hectic, prepare everything the night before, take it out so the crock warms up to room temperature when you first get up in the morning, then plug it in and turn it on as you're leaving the house.

If you want to make something that has a short cook time and you're going to be gone longer than that, cook it the night before and refrigerate it for the next day. Warm it up when you get home. Or, cook those recipes on the weekend when you know you'll be home and eat them later in the week.

Slow Cooking Tips and Tricks and Other Things You May Not Know

- Slow cookers tend to work best when they're ⅔ to ¾ of the way full. You may need to increase the cooking time if you've exceeded that amount, or reduce it if you've put in less than that. If you're going to exceed that limit, it would be best to reduce the recipe, or split it between two slow cookers. (Remember how I suggested owning at least two or three slow cookers?)

- Keep your veggies on the bottom. That puts them in more direct contact with the heat. The fuller your slow cooker, the longer it will take its contents to cook. Also, the more densely packed the cooker's contents are, the longer they will take to cook. And finally, the larger the chunks of meat or vegetables, the more time they will need to cook.

- Keep the lid on! Every time you take a peek, you lose 20 minutes of cooking time. Please take this into consideration each time you lift the lid! I know, some of you can't help yourself and are going to lift anyway. Just don't forget to tack on 20 minutes to your cook time for each time you peeked!

- Sometimes it's beneficial to remove the lid. If you'd like your dish to thicken a bit, take the lid off during the last half hour to hour of cooking time.

- If you have a big slow cooker (7- to 8-quart), you can cook a small batch in it by putting the recipe ingredients into an oven-safe baking dish or baking pan and then placing that into the cooker's crock. First, put a trivet or some metal jar rings on the bottom of the crock, and then set your dish or pan on top of them. Or a loaf pan may "hook onto" the top ridges of the crock belonging to a large oval cooker and hang there straight and securely, "baking" a cake or quick bread. Cover the cooker and flip it on.

- The outside of your slow cooker will be hot! Please remember to keep it out of reach of children, and keep that in mind for yourself as well!

- Get yourself a quick-read meat thermometer and use it! This helps remove the question of whether or not your meat is fully cooked, and helps prevent you from overcooking your meat as well.
  - Internal Cooking Temperatures: Beef—125–130°F (rare); 140–145°F (medium); 160°F (well-done)
  - Pork—140–145°F (rare); 145–150°F (medium); 160°F (well-done)
  - Turkey and Chicken—165°F
  - Frozen meat: The basic rule of thumb is, don't put frozen meat into the slow cooker. The meat does not reach the proper internal temperature in time. This especially applies to thick cuts of meat! Proceed with caution!

- Add fresh herbs 10 minutes before the end of the cooking time to maximize their flavor.
- If your recipe calls for cooked pasta, add it 10 minutes before the end of the cooking time if the cooker is on High; 30 minutes before the end of the cooking time if it's on Low. Then the pasta won't get mushy.
- If your recipe calls for sour cream or cream, stir it in 5 minutes before the end of the cooking time. You want it to heat but not boil or simmer.
  - Approximate Slow Cooker Temperatures (Remember, each slow cooker is different):
  - High—212°F–300°F
  - Low—170°F–200°F
  - Simmer—185°F
  - Warm—165°F
- Cooked beans freeze well. Store them in freezer bags (squeeze the air out first) or freezer boxes. Cooked and dried bean measurements:
  - 16-oz. can, drained = about 1¾ cups beans
  - 19-oz. can, drained = about 2 cups beans
  - 1 lb. dried beans (about 2½ cups) = 5 cups cooked beans

What Is an Instant Pot?

In short, an Instant Pot is a digital pressure cooker that also has multiple other functions. Not only can it be used as a pressure cooker, but depending on which model Instant Pot you have, you can set it to things like sauté, cook rice, grains, porridge, soup/stew, beans/chili, porridge, meat, poultry, cake, eggs, yogurt. You can use the Instant Pot to steam or slow cook or even set it manually. Because the Instant Pot has so many functions, it takes away the need for multiple appliances on your counter and allows you to use fewer pots and pans.

Getting Started with Your Instant Pot

Get to Know Your Instant Pot . . .

The very first thing most Instant Pot owners do is called the water test. It helps you get to know your Instant Pot a bit, familiarizes you with it, and might even take a bit of your apprehension away (because if you're anything like me, I was scared to death to use it).

Step 1: Plug in your Instant Pot. This may seem obvious to some, but when we're nervous about using a new appliance, sometimes we forget things like this.

Step 2: Make sure the inner pot is inserted in the cooker. You should *never* attempt to cook anything in your device without the inner pot, or you will ruin your Instant Pot. Food should never come into contact with the actual housing unit.

Step 3: The inner pot has lines for each cup. Fill the inner pot with water until it reaches the 3-cup line.

Step 4: Check the sealing ring to be sure it's secure and in place. You should not be able to move it around. If it's not in place properly, you may experience issues with the pot letting out a lot of steam while cooking, or not coming to pressure.

Step 5: Seal the lid. There is an arrow on the lid between and "open" and "close." There is also an arrow on the top of the base of the Instant Pot between a picture of a locked lock and an unlocked lock. Line those arrows up, then turn the lid toward the picture of the lock (left).You will hear a noise that will indicate the lid is locked. If you do not hear a noise, it's not locked. Try it again.

Step 6: *Always* check to see if the steam valve on top of the lid is turned to "sealing." If it's not on "sealing" and is on "venting," it will not be able to come to pressure.

Step 7: Press the Steam button and use the +/- arrow to set it to 2 minutes. Once it's at the desired time, you don't need to press anything else. In a few seconds, the Instant Pot will begin all on its own. For those of us with digital slow cookers, we have a tendency to look for the Start button, but there isn't one on the Instant Pot.

Step 8: Now you wait for the "magic" to happen! The cooking will begin once the device comes to pressure. This can take anywhere from 5 to 30 minutes, in my experience. Then, you will see the countdown happen (from the time you set it for). After that, the Instant Pot will beep, which means your meal is done!

Step 9: Your Instant Pot will now automatically switch to "warm" and begin a count of how many minutes it's been on warm. The next part is where you either wait for the NPR, or natural pressure release (the pressure releases on its own), or do what's called a QR, or quick release (you manually release the pressure). Which method you choose depends on what you're cooking, but in this case, you can choose either, because it's just water. For NPR, you will wait for the lever to move all the way back over to "venting" and watch the pinion (float valve) next to the lever. It will be flush with the lid when at full pressure and will drop when the pressure is done releasing. If you choose QR, be very careful not to have your hands over the vent, as the steam is very hot and you can burn yourself.

The Three Most Important Buttons You Need to Know About

You will find the majority of recipes will use the following three buttons:

Manual/Pressure Cook: Some older models tend to say "Manual," and the newer models seem to say "Pressure Cook." They mean the same thing. From here, you use the +/- button to change the cook time. After several seconds, the Instant Pot will begin its process. The exact name of this button will vary on your model of Instant Pot.

Sauté: Many recipes will have you sauté vegetables, or brown meat before beginning the pressure cooking process. For this setting, you will not use the lid of the Instant Pot.

Keep Warm/Cancel: This may just be the most important button on the Instant Pot. When you forget to use the +/- buttons to change the time for a recipe, or you press a wrong button, you can hit "keep warm/cancel" and it will turn your Instant Pot off for you.

What Do All the Buttons Do?

With so many buttons, it's hard to remember what each one does or means. You can use this as a quick guide in a pinch.

Soup/Broth: This button cooks at high pressure for 30 minutes. It can be adjusted using the +/- buttons to cook more, for 40 minutes, or less, for 20 minutes.

Meat/Stew: This button cooks at high pressure for 35 minutes. It can be adjusted using the +/- buttons to cook more, for 45 minutes, or less, for 20 minutes.

Bean/Chili: This button cooks at high pressure for 30 minutes. It can be adjusted using the +/- buttons to cook more, for 40 minutes, or less, for 25 minutes.

Poultry: This button cooks at high pressure for 15 minutes. It can be adjusted using the +/- buttons to cook more, for 30 minutes, or less, for 5 minutes.

Rice: This button cooks at low pressure and is the only fully automatic program. It is for cooking white rice and will automatically adjust the cooking time depending on the amount of water and rice in the cooking pot.

Multigrain: This button cooks at high pressure for 40 minutes. It can be adjusted using the +/- buttons to cook more, for 45 minutes of warm water soaking time and 60 minutes pressure cooking time, or less, for 20 minutes.

Porridge: This button cooks at high pressure for 20 minutes. It can be adjusted using the +/- buttons to cook more, for 30 minutes, or less, for 15 minutes.

Steam: This button cooks at high pressure for 10 minutes. It can be adjusted using the +/- buttons to cook more, for 15 minutes, or less, for 3 minutes. Always use a rack or steamer basket with this function, because it heats at full power continuously while it's coming to pressure, and you do not want food in direct contact with the bottom of the pressure cooking pot or it will burn. Once it reaches pressure, the steam button regulates pressure by cycling on and off, similar to the other pressure buttons.

Less | Normal | More: Adjust between the *Less | Normal | More* settings by pressing the same cooking function button repeatedly until you get to the desired setting. (Older versions use the *Adjust* button.)

+/- Buttons: Adjust the cook time up [+] or down [-]. (On newer models, you can also press and hold [-] or [+] for 3 seconds to turn sound OFF or ON.)

Cake: This button cooks at high pressure for 30 minutes. It can be adjusted using the +/- buttons to cook more, for 40 minutes, or less, for 25 minutes.

Egg: This button cooks at high pressure for 5 minutes. It can be adjusted using the +/- buttons to cook more, for 6 minutes, or less, for 4 minutes.

Instant Pot Tips and Tricks and Other Things You May Not Know

- Never attempt to cook directly in the Instant Pot without the inner pot!

- Once you set the time, you can walk away. It will show the time you set it to, then will change to the word "on" while the pressure builds. Once the Instant Pot has come to pressure, you will once again see the time you set it for. It will count down from there.

- Always make sure the sealing ring is securely in place. If it shows signs of wear or tear, it needs to be replaced.

- Have a sealing ring for savory recipes and a separate sealing ring for sweet recipes. Many people report their desserts tasting like a roast (or another savory food) if they try to use the same sealing ring for all recipes.

- The stainless steel rack (trivet) the Instant Pot comes with can used to keep food from being completely submerged in liquid, like baked potatoes or ground beef. It can also be used to set another pot on, for pot-in-pot cooking.

- If you use warm or hot liquid instead of cold liquid, you may need to adjust the cooking time, or the food may not come out done.

- Always double-check to see that the valve on the lid is set to "sealing" and not "venting" when you first lock the lid. This will save you from the Instant Pot not coming to pressure.

- Use Natural Pressure Release for tougher cuts of meat, recipes with high starch (like rice or grains), and recipes with a high volume of liquid. This means you let the Instant Pot naturally release pressure. The little bobbin will fall once pressure is released completely.

- Use Quick Release for more delicate cuts of meat, such as seafood and chicken breasts, and for steaming vegetables. This means you manually turn the vent (being careful not to put your hand over the vent) to release the pressure. The little bobbin will fall once pressure is released completely.

- Make sure there is a clear pathway for the steam to release. The last thing you want is to ruin the bottom of your cupboards with all that steam.

- You *must* use liquid in the Instant Pot. The *minimum* amount of liquid you should have in the inner pot is ½ cup, but most recipes work best with at least 1 cup.

- Do *not* overfill the Instant Pot! It should only be ½ full for rice or beans (food that expands greatly when cooked), or 2/3 of the way full for almost everything else. Do not fill it to the max fill line.

- In this book, the Cook Time *does not* take into account the amount of time it will take the Instant Pot to come to pressure, or the amount of time it will take the Instant Pot to release pressure. Be aware of this when choosing a recipe to make.

- If the Instant Pot is not coming to pressure, it's usually because the sealing ring is not on properly, or the vent is not set to "sealing."
- The more liquid, or the colder the ingredients, the longer it will take for the Instant Pot to come to pressure.
- Always make sure that the Instant Pot is dry before inserting the inner pot, and make sure the inner pot is dry before inserting it into the Instant Pot.
- Use a binder clip to hold the inner pot tight against the outer pot when sautéing and stirring. This will keep the pot from "spinning" in the base.
- Doubling a recipe does not change the cook time, but instead it will take longer to come up to pressure.
- You do not always need to double the liquid when doubling a recipe. Depending on what you're making, more liquid may make the food too watery. Use your best judgment.
- When using the slow cooker function, use the following chart:

Slow Cooker	Instant Pot
Warm	Less or Low
Low	Normal or Medium
High	More or High

Instant Pot Accessories

For this particular book, no accessories are needed! However, most Instant Pots come with a stainless steel trivet. Below, you will find a list of accessories that are frequently used in most Fix-It and Forget-It Instant Pot cookbooks. These accessories can be purchased in-store or online.

- Steamer basket—stainless steel or silicone
- 7-inch nonstick or silicone springform cake pan or
- Sling or trivet with handles
- 1½-quart round baking dish
- Silicone egg molds

Soups

Chicken Soups

Chicken and Vegetable Soup with Rice

Hope Comerford, Clinton Township, MI

Makes 6–8 servings
Prep. Time: 20 minutes ♣ Cooking Time: 6½–7½ hours ♣ Ideal slow-cooker size: 3-qt.

1½–2 lb. boneless, skinless chicken breasts

1½ cups chopped carrots

1½ cups chopped red onion

2 Tbsp. garlic powder

1 Tbsp. onion powder

2 tsp. kosher salt

¼ tsp. celery seed

¼ tsp. paprika

⅛ tsp. pepper

1 dried bay leaf

8 cups no-salt chicken stock

1 cup fresh green beans

3 cups cooked rice

1. Place chicken into the bottom of crock, then add rest of the remaining ingredients, except green beans and rice.

2. Cover and cook on Low for 6–7 hours.

3. Remove chicken and chop into bite-sized cubes. Place chicken back into crock and add in green beans. Cover and cook another 30 minutes.

4. To serve, place approximately ½ cup of the cooked rice into each bowl and ladle soup over top of the rice.

Italiano Chicken, Rice, and Tomato Soup

SLOW COOKER

Jane Geigley, Lancaster, PA

Makes 6 servings
Prep. Time: 30 minutes   Cooking Time: 4–6 hours   Ideal slow-cooker size: 4-qt.

½ cup chopped onion

2 Tbsp. butter, softened

½ tsp. paprika

½ tsp. basil

⅛ tsp. garlic powder

8-oz. brick cream cheese, softened

1¼ cups milk

2 (10¾-oz.) cans tomato soup

2 (16-oz.) cans whole tomatoes, undrained

1 cup instant rice

2 cups cooked chopped chicken

1 cup shredded mozzarella cheese

1. In a stand mixer, mix the first 9 ingredients. Beat until smooth. Pour into the slow cooker.

2. Stir in rice and chicken.

3. Cover and cook on Low for 4–6 hours. Add the shredded cheese at the very end, just before serving.

Creamy Chicken Wild Rice Soup

INSTANT POT

Vonnie Oyer, Hubbard, OR

Makes 4–6 servings

Prep. Time: 15 minutes ♣ *Cooking Time: 15 minutes* ♣ *Recommended Instant Pot size: 6-qt.*

2 Tbsp. butter

½ cup diced yellow onion

¾ cup diced carrots

¾ cup sliced mushrooms (about 3–4 mushrooms)

½ lb. chicken breast, diced into 1-inch cubes

6.2-oz. box Ben's Original™ Long Grain & Wild Rice Fast Cook

2 (14-oz.) cans chicken broth

1 cup milk

1 cup half-and-half

2 oz. cream cheese

2 Tbsp. cornstarch

1. Select the Sauté feature and add the butter, onion, carrots, and mushrooms to the inner pot. Sauté for about 5 minutes until onions are translucent and soft.

2. Add the cubed chicken and seasoning packet from the Ben's Original™ box and stir to combine.

3. Add the wild rice and chicken broth. Select Manual, high pressure, then lock the lid and make sure the vent is set to sealing. Set the time for 5 minutes.

4. After the cooking time ends, allow it to stay on Keep Warm for 5 minutes and then quick release the pressure.

5. Remove the lid; change the setting to the Sauté function again.

6. Add the milk, half-and-half, and cream cheese. Stir to melt.

7. In a small bowl mix the cornstarch with a little bit of water to dissolve, then add to the soup to thicken.

Chicken Tortilla Soup

Becky Fixel, Grosse Pointe Farms, MI

Makes 10–12 servings
Prep. Time: 5 minutes ⚬ Cooking Time: 7–8 hours ⚬ Ideal slow-cooker size: 5-qt.

2 lb. boneless, skinless chicken breast

32 oz. chicken stock

14 oz. salsa verde

10-oz. can diced tomatoes with lime juice

15-oz. can sweet corn, drained

1 Tbsp. minced garlic

1 small onion, diced

1 Tbsp. chili pepper

½ tsp. fresh ground pepper

½ tsp. salt

½ tsp. oregano

1 Tbsp. dried jalapeño slices

1. Add all ingredients to your slow cooker.

2. Cook on Low for 7–8 hours.

3. Approximately 30 minutes before the end, remove your chicken and shred it into small pieces.

Serving suggestion:

Top with a dollop of nonfat plain Greek yogurt, shredded cheese, fresh jalapeños, or fresh cilantro.

Chicken Chickpea Tortilla Soup

Hope Comerford, Clinton Township, MI

Makes 4–6 servings
Prep. Time: 5 minutes 🞂 Cooking Time: 6 hours 🞂 Ideal slow-cooker size: 4-qt.

2 boneless, skinless chicken breasts

2 (14½-oz.) cans petite diced tomatoes

15-oz. can garbanzo beans (chickpeas), drained

6 cups chicken stock

1 onion, chopped

4-oz. can diced green chilies

1 tsp. cilantro

3–4 cloves garlic, minced

1 tsp. sea salt

1 tsp. pepper

1 tsp. cumin

1 tsp. paprika

1. Place all ingredients in slow cooker.

2. Cover and cook on Low for 6 hours.

3. Use two forks to pull chicken into shreds.

Serving suggestion:

Serve with a small dollop of nonfat Greek yogurt, a little shredded cheddar, and some baked blue corn tortilla chips.

Southwest Chicken and White Bean Soup

SLOW COOKER

Karen Ceneviva, Seymour, CT

Makes 6 servings
Prep. Time: 15 minutes ⚭ *Cooking Time: 4–10 hours* ⚭ *Ideal slow-cooker size: 3½-qt.*

1 Tbsp. vegetable oil

1 lb. boneless, skinless chicken breasts, cut into 1-inch cubes

1¾ cups chicken broth

1 cup chunky salsa

3 cloves garlic, minced

2 Tbsp. cumin

15½-oz. can small white beans, rinsed and drained

1 cup frozen corn

1 large onion, chopped

1. Heat oil in 10-inch skillet over medium to high heat. Add chicken and cook until it is well browned on all sides. Stir frequently to prevent sticking.

2. Mix broth, salsa, garlic, cumin, beans, corn, and onion in slow cooker. Add chicken. Stir well.

3. Cover. Cook 8–10 hours on Low or 4–5 hours on High.

Chicken Noodle Soup

Colleen Heatwole, Burton, MI

Makes 6–8 servings
Prep. Time: 15 minutes ⚜ Cooking Time: 4 minutes ⚜ Recommended Instant Pot size: 6-qt.

2 Tbsp. butter

1 Tbsp. oil

1 medium onion, diced

2 large carrots, diced

3 ribs celery, diced

3 cloves garlic, minced

1 tsp. thyme

1 tsp. oregano

1 tsp. basil

8 cups chicken broth

2 cups cubed cooked chicken

8 oz. medium egg noodles

1 cup frozen peas (thaw while preparing soup)

Salt and pepper to taste

1. In the inner pot of the Instant Pot, melt the butter with oil on the Sauté function.

2. Add onion, carrots, and celery with large pinch of salt and continue cooking on sauté until soft, about 5 minutes, stirring frequently.

3. Add garlic, thyme, oregano, and basil and sauté an additional minute.

4. Add broth, cooked chicken, and noodles, stirring to combine all ingredients.

5. Put lid on the Instant Pot and set vent to sealing. Select Manual high pressure and add 4 minutes.

6. When time is up do a quick (manual) release of the pressure.

7. Add thawed peas, stir, adjust seasoning with salt and pepper, and serve.

Note from the cook:

You can also prepare chicken for this recipe in the Instant Pot, but for this recipe, I usually use leftovers.

Chicken and Corn Soup

Eleanor Larson, Glen Lyon, PA

Makes 4–6 servings
Prep. Time: 15 minutes   &   Cooking Time: 8–9 hours   &   Ideal slow-cooker size: 4-qt.

2 whole boneless, skinless chicken
breasts, cubed

1 onion, chopped

1 clove garlic, minced

2 carrots, sliced

2 ribs celery, chopped

2 medium potatoes, cubed

1 tsp. mixed dried herbs

⅓ cup tomato sauce

12-oz. can cream-style corn

14-oz. can whole kernel corn

3 cups chicken stock

¼ cup chopped Italian parsley

1 tsp. salt

¼ tsp. pepper

1. Combine all ingredients except parsley, salt, and pepper in slow cooker.

2. Cover. Cook on Low 8–9 hours, or until chicken is tender.

3. Add parsley and seasonings 30 minutes before serving.

Black Bean Soup with Chicken and Salsa

Hope Comerford, Clinton Township, MI

Makes 4–6 servings

Prep. Time: 10 minutes 🍃 Cooking Time: 6–8 hours 🍃 Ideal slow-cooker size: 5- to 6-qt.

4 cups chicken broth

1 large boneless, skinless chicken breast

2 (15-oz.) cans black beans, rinsed and drained

16-oz. jar salsa

1 cup frozen corn

1 cup sliced fresh mushrooms

½ red onion, chopped

1 jalapeño pepper (whole)

1½ tsp. cumin

Salt and pepper to taste

Optional Toppings:

Shredded cheese

Sour cream

Cilantro

Avocado

1. Place all ingredients except the toppings in slow cooker. Stir.

2. Cover and cook on Low for 6–8 hours.

3. Remove the chicken and shred between two forks. Replace back in the soup and stir.

Variation:

You may chop up the jalapeño for extra heat. Leaving it whole provides the flavor without the heat.

Serving suggestion:

Serve garnished with the optional toppings.

Buffalo Chicken Wing Soup

SLOW COOKER

Mary Lynn Miller, Reinholds, PA
Donna Neiter, Wausau, WI
Joette Droz, Kalona, IA

Makes 8 servings
Prep. Time: 10 minutes ❧ Cooking Time: 4–5 hours ❧ Ideal slow-cooker size: 3-qt.

6 cups milk

3 (10¾-oz.) cans condensed cream of chicken soup, undiluted

3 cups (about 1 lb.) shredded or cubed cooked chicken

1 cup sour cream

1–8 Tbsp. hot pepper sauce, according to your preference for heat

1. Combine milk and soups in slow cooker until smooth.

2. Stir in chicken.

3. Cover and cook on Low 3¾–4¾ hours.

4. Fifteen minutes before serving, stir in sour cream and hot sauce.

5. Cover and continue cooking just until bubbly.

Chicken Cheddar Broccoli Soup

Maria Shevlin, Sicklerville, NJ

Makes 4–6 servings

Prep. Time: 15 minutes ☙ Cooking Time: 15 minutes ☙ Recommended Instant Pot size: 6-qt.

1 lb. raw chicken breast, thinly sliced and cut into pieces

1 lb. fresh broccoli, chopped

½ cup onion, chopped

2 cloves garlic, minced

1 cup shredded carrots

½ cup finely chopped celery

¼ cup finely chopped red bell pepper

3 cups chicken bone broth

½ tsp. salt

¼ tsp. black pepper

½ tsp. garlic powder

1 tsp. parsley flakes

Pinch red pepper flakes

2 cups heavy cream

8 oz. freshly shredded cheddar cheese

2 Tbsp. Frank's® RedHot® Original Cayenne Pepper Sauce

1. Place chicken, broccoli, chopped onion, garlic, carrots, celery, bell pepper, chicken broth, and seasonings in the pot and stir to mix.

2. Secure the lid and make sure vent is at sealing. Place on Manual at high pressure for 15 minutes.

3. Manually release the pressure when cook time us up, remove lid, and stir in heavy cream.

4. Place pot on sauté setting until it all comes to a low boil, approximately 5 minutes.

5. Stir in cheese and the hot sauce.

6. Turn off the pot as soon as you add the cheese and give it a stir.

7. Continue to stir until the cheese is melted.

Serving suggestion:

Serve it up with slice or two of garlic bread or bread of your choice.

Turkey Soups

Turkey Rosemary Veggie Soup

SLOW COOKER

Willard E. Roth, Elkhart, IN

Makes 8 servings

Prep. Time: 30 minutes ♣ Cooking Time: 8 hours ♣ Ideal slow-cooker size: 6-qt.

1 lb. 99% fat-free ground turkey

3 parsley stalks with leaves, sliced

3 green onions, chopped

3 medium carrots, unpeeled, sliced

3 medium potatoes, unpeeled, sliced

3 celery ribs with leaves, sliced

3 small onions, sliced

16-oz. can whole-kernel corn, undrained

16-oz. can green beans, undrained

16-oz. can low-sodium diced Italian-style tomatoes

3 cans water

3 packets dry Herb-Ox® vegetable bouillon

1 Tbsp. dried rosemary

1. Brown turkey with parsley and green onions in nonstick skillet. Drain. Pour into slow cooker sprayed with nonstick spray.

2. Add vegetables, water, dry vegetable broth, and rosemary.

3. Cover. Cook on Low 8 hours, or until vegetables are done to your liking.

Turkey Peasant Soup

Alice Valine, Elma, NY

Makes 8 servings

Prep. Time: 11 minutes 🐚 *Cook Time: 5 minutes* 🐚 *Recommended Instant Pot size: 6-qt.*

2 Tbsp. olive oil

1 medium onion, chopped

2–3 cloves garlic, minced

½ lb. bulk turkey sausage

2 (15-oz.) cans cannellini beans, rinsed and drained

2 (14½-oz.) cans no-salt-added diced tomatoes

4 cups low-sodium chicken or vegetable stock

2 tsp. Italian seasoning

3 medium zucchini, sliced

4 cups fresh spinach leaves, chopped, or whole-leaf baby spinach

Shredded Parmesan or Romano cheese, *optional*

1. Set the Instant Pot to Sauté and heat the olive oil in the inner pot.

2. Sauté the onion and garlic for about 3 minutes. Push it to the outer edges and brown the turkey sausage for an additional 5 to 8 minutes.

3. Press Cancel and add the cannellini beans, diced tomatoes, chicken stock, Italian seasoning, and zucchini.

4. Secure the lid and set the vent to sealing.

5. Manually set the cook time for 5 minutes on high pressure.

6. When the cook time is over, let the pressure release naturally for 10 minutes, then manually release the remaining pressure.

7. When the pin drops, remove the lid and stir in the spinach. Allow the spinach to wilt.

8. Serve each bowl with an optional sprinkle of shredded Parmesan or Romano cheese.

Turkey Zucchini Soup

Wilma J. Haberkamp, Fairbank, IA

Makes 8 servings

Prep. Time: 20 minutes   ⚜   Cooking Time: 2½–3½ hours   ⚜   Ideal slow-cooker size: 4-qt.

8- or 10-oz. pkg. frozen green beans

2 cups zucchini, thinly sliced

2 cups turkey, cooked and chopped

8-oz. can tomato sauce

½ cup chopped onions

1 Tbsp. instant chicken bouillon granules

1 tsp. Worcestershire sauce

¼ tsp. salt

½ tsp. dried savory, crushed

Dash black pepper

4 cups water

3 oz. light cream cheese, softened

1. Thaw green beans. If you're in a hurry, place them in a strainer and run hot water over them.

2. Combine beans, zucchini, turkey, tomato sauce, onions, bouillon, Worcestershire sauce, salt, savory, black pepper, and water in slow cooker.

3. Cook on High 2–3 hours.

4. Blend 1 cup hot soup with cream cheese. Return to slow cooker and stir well. Cook until hot, about 20 minutes.

Turkey Frame Soup

Joyce Zuercher, Hesston, KS

Makes 6–8 servings
Prep. Time: 40 minutes   ♣   Cooking Time: 3–4 hours   ♣   Ideal slow-cooker size: 6-qt.

2–3 cups cooked and cut-up turkey*

3 qt. turkey or chicken broth

1 onion, diced

½–¾ tsp. salt, or to taste

16-oz. can diced tomatoes

1 Tbsp. low-sodium chicken bouillon granules

1 tsp. dried thyme

⅛ tsp. pepper

1½ tsp. dried oregano

4 cups chopped fresh vegetables—any combination of sliced celery, carrots, onions, rutabaga, broccoli, cauliflower, mushrooms, and more

1½ cups uncooked gluten-free noodles

1. Place turkey, broth, onion, salt, tomatoes, bouillon granules, thyme, pepper, oregano, and vegetables into slow cooker. Stir.

2. Cover. Cook on Low 3–4 hours, or until vegetables are nearly done.

3. Fifteen to 30 minutes before serving time, stir in noodles. Cover. Cook on Low. If noodles are thin and small, they'll cook in 15 minutes or less. If heavier, they may need 30 minutes to become tender.

4. Stir well before serving.

---

* If you've got a big turkey frame, and you know it's got some good meaty morsels on it, here's what to do: Break it up enough to fit into a Dutch oven. Add 3 qt. water, 1 onion, quartered, and 2 tsp. salt. Cover and simmer 1½ hours. Remove turkey bones from Dutch oven and allow to cool. Then debone and chop meat coarsely. Discard bones and skin. Strain broth. Begin with Step 1 above!

Ground Turkey Soup

SLOW COOKER

Betty K. Drescher, Quakertown, PA

Makes 12 servings
Prep. Time: 20–30 minutes ♣ Cooking Time: 8–9 hours ♣ Ideal slow-cooker size: 5- or 6-qt.

1 lb. ground turkey
1 cup chopped onions
1 clove garlic, minced
15-oz. can kidney beans, drained
1 cup sliced carrots
1 cup sliced celery
¼ cup long-grain rice, uncooked
1 qt. low-sodium diced Italian tomatoes
2 cups fresh or frozen green beans
1 tsp. parsley flakes
½ green bell pepper, chopped
1 tsp. salt
⅛ tsp. black pepper
1 Tbsp. Worcestershire sauce
1 bay leaf
3 cups water

1. Brown turkey in a large nonstick skillet.

2. Combine with remaining ingredients in slow cooker.

3. Cover. Cook on Low 8–9 hours. Remove bay leaf before serving.

Taco Soup

Marla Folkerts, Holland, OH

Makes 6 servings
Prep. Time: 20 minutes ⚘ Cooking Time: 4–6 hours ⚘ Ideal slow-cooker size: 3½- or 4-qt.

Soup:

1 lb. lean ground turkey or ground beef

1 medium-sized onion, chopped

1 medium-sized green bell pepper, chopped

1 envelope dry reduced-sodium taco seasoning

½ cup water

4 cups reduced-sodium vegetable juice

1 cup chunky salsa

Toppings:

¾ cup shredded lettuce

6 Tbsp. fresh tomato, chopped

6 Tbsp. cheddar cheese, shredded

¼ cup green onions or chives, chopped

¼ cup sour cream or plain yogurt

Tortilla or corn chips

1. Brown meat with onion in nonstick skillet. Drain.

2. Combine all soup ingredients in slow cooker.

3. Cover. Cook on Low 4–6 hours.

4. Serve with your choice of toppings.

Turkey Meatball Soup

Mary Ann Lefever, Lancaster, PA

Makes 8 servings
Prep. Time: 30 minutes ⚶ Cooking Time: 8 hours ⚶ Ideal slow-cooker size: 5- to 6-qt.

4–5 large carrots, chopped

10 cups chicken broth

¾ lb. escarole, washed and cut into bite-sized pieces

1 lb. ground turkey, uncooked

1 medium onion, chopped

2 large eggs, beaten

½ cup Italian bread crumbs

½ cup freshly grated Parmesan, plus more for serving

1 tsp. salt

¼ tsp. pepper

1. In slow cooker, combine carrots and broth.

2. Stir in escarole.

3. Cover. Cook on Low 4 hours.

4. Combine turkey, onion, eggs, bread crumbs, ½ cup Parmesan cheese, salt, and pepper in good-sized bowl. Mix well and shape into 1-inch balls. Drop carefully into soup.

5. Cover cooker. Cook on Low 4 more hours, or just until meatballs and vegetables are cooked through.

6. Serve hot sprinkled with extra Parmesan cheese.

Tip:

If you wish, you can substitute 3 cups cut-up cooked turkey for the ground turkey meatballs.

Pork Soups

Italian Vegetable Soup

Patti Boston, Newark, OH

Makes 6 servings
Prep. Time: 20 minutes ⚬ Cook Time: 10 minutes ⚬ Recommended Instant Pot size: 6-qt.

3 small carrots, sliced

1 small onion, chopped

2 small potatoes, diced

2 Tbsp. chopped parsley

1 clove garlic, minced

3 tsp. sodium-free beef bouillon powder

1¼ tsp. dried basil

¼ tsp. pepper

16-oz. can red kidney beans, undrained

14½-oz. can stewed tomatoes, with juice

1 cup diced, extra-lean, lower-sodium cooked ham

3 cups water

1. In the inner pot of the Instant Pot, layer the carrots, onion, potatoes, parsley, garlic, beef bouillon, basil, pepper, kidney beans, stewed tomatoes, and ham. Do not stir. Add the water.

2. Secure the lid and set the vent to sealing. Manually set the cook time for 10 minutes.

3. When the cook time is over, let the pressure release naturally for 2 minutes, then manually release the remaining pressure.

Cabbage Sausage Soup

Karen Waggoner, Joplin, MO

Makes 8 servings
Prep. Time: 20–25 minutes & Cooking Time: 5¼–6¼ hours & Ideal slow-cooker size: 5-qt.

4 cups low-sodium chicken broth

1 medium-sized head of cabbage, chopped

2 medium-sized onions, chopped

½ lb. fully cooked sausage, halved lengthwise and sliced

½ cup all-purpose flour

¼ tsp. black pepper

1 cup milk

1. Combine chicken broth, cabbage, onions, and sausage in slow cooker.

2. Cover. Cook on High 5–6 hours, or until cabbage is tender.

3. Mix flour and black pepper in bowl.

4. Gradually add milk, stirring until smooth.

5. Gradually stir into hot soup.

6. Cook, stirring occasionally for about 15 minutes, until soup is thickened. Serve.

Tip:

Add salt to each bowl if needed or wanted after tasting. It's a great way to control the sodium level of your recipe.

Kielbasa Soup

Bernice M. Gnidovec, Streator, IL

Makes 8 servings
Prep. Time: 10 minutes   ⚮   Cooking Time: 12 hours   ⚮   Ideal slow-cooker size: 8-qt.

16-oz. pkg. frozen mixed vegetables, or your choice of vegetables

6-oz. can tomato paste

1 medium onion, chopped

3 medium potatoes, diced

1½ lb. kielbasa, cut into ¼-inch pieces

4 qt. water

1. Combine all ingredients in large slow cooker.

2. Cover. Cook on Low 12 hours.

Hearty Potato Sauerkraut Soup

SLOW COOKER

Kathy Hertzler, Lancaster, PA

Makes 6–8 servings

Prep. Time: 15–20 minutes ⚶ *Cooking Time: 10–12 hours* ⚶ *Ideal slow-cooker size: 4-qt.*

4 cups chicken broth

10¾-oz. can cream of mushroom soup

16-oz. can sauerkraut, rinsed and drained

8 oz. fresh mushrooms, sliced

1 medium potato, cubed

2 medium carrots, peeled and sliced

2 ribs celery, chopped

2 lb. Polish kielbasa (smoked), cubed

2½ cups chopped, cooked chicken

2 Tbsp. vinegar

2 tsp. dried dill weed

1½ tsp. pepper

1. Combine all ingredients in large slow cooker.

2. Cover. Cook on Low 10–12 hours.

3. If necessary, skim fat before serving.

Sausage White Bean Soup

SLOW COOKER

Christie Anne Detamore-Hunsberger, Harrisonburg, VA

Makes 8 servings
Prep. Time: 30–45 minutes 🌿 Cooking Time: 3 hours 🌿 Ideal slow-cooker size: 4-qt.

⅓ lb. Italian turkey sausage, sweet or hot, cut in ½-inch-thick slices

½ cup water, or more

1 large onion, diced

2 cloves garlic, minced

5 carrots, grated

3 stalks celery, chopped

2–2½ qt. low-sodium chicken broth

3–4 tsp. low-sodium chicken bouillon granules

1 tsp. vegetable seasoning blend, your choice

½ tsp. dried oregano

¼ tsp. pepper

3 (15-oz.) cans white beans, rinsed and drained

3 cups frozen spinach, thawed

2 Tbsp. parsley

1. Brown sausage in skillet in ½ cup water over medium to high heat. Cover. Check and stir after 10 minutes or so to make sure sausage isn't cooking dry and burning. Add more water if needed and continue stirring until browned on all sides.

2. Remove sausage to slow cooker, reserving drippings.

3. Sauté onion, garlic, carrots, and celery in drippings in skillet until tender. Place vegetables in slow cooker.

4. Add chicken broth and granules, all seasonings, and beans. Stir well.

5. Cook on Low 3 hours.

6. Squeeze excess liquid out of thawed spinach. Add to slow cooker for last 20–30 minutes of cooking time.

7. Garnish with parsley.

The Best Bean and Ham Soup

Hope Comerford, Clinton Township, MI

Makes 8–10 servings
Prep. Time: 8 minutes & Soaking Time: 8 hours or overnight
Cooking Time: 8–12 hours & Ideal slow-cooker size: 7-qt.

1 meaty ham bone or shank
1 lb. dry navy beans
1 cup chopped onions
2 cloves garlic, minced
1 cup chopped celery
¼ cup chopped parsley
1 Tbsp. sea salt
1 tsp. pepper
1 tsp. nutmeg
1 tsp. oregano
1 tsp. basil
2 bay leaves
8 cups low-sodium chicken stock
6–8 cups water

1. Place the ham bone in the bottom of the crock and pour all of the remaining ingredients into the crock around it, ending with the water. You'll want to make sure you've covered the ham bone with water.

2. Cover and cook on Low for 8–12 hours. Remove bay leaves before serving.

Black Bean and Ham Soup

Colleen Heatwole, Burton, MI

Makes 4 servings
Prep. Time: 30 minutes ☙ *Cooking Time: 6–8 hours* ☙ *Ideal slow-cooker size: 5-qt.*

2 cups chopped carrots

1 cup chopped celery

2 cloves garlic, minced

1 medium onion, chopped

2 (15½-oz.) cans black beans, undrained

2 (14½-oz.) cans chicken or vegetable broth

15-oz. can crushed tomatoes

1½ tsp. dried basil

½ tsp. dried oregano

½ tsp. ground cumin

½ tsp. chili powder

¼ tsp. hot pepper sauce

1 cup diced cooked ham

1. Combine all ingredients in slow cooker.

2. Cover and cook on Low 6–8 hours or until vegetables are tender.

Grandma's Barley Soup

Andrea O'Neil, Fairfield, CT

Makes 10–12 servings
Prep. Time: 10 minutes ❧ *Cooking Time: 6–8 hours* ❧ *Ideal slow-cooker size: 4- or 5-qt.*

2 smoked ham hocks
4 carrots, sliced
4 potatoes, cubed
1 cup dry lima beans
1 cup low-sodium tomato paste
1½–2 cups cooked barley
Salt to taste

1. Combine all ingredients in slow cooker, except salt.

2. Cover with water.

3. Cover. Simmer on Low 6–8 hours, or until both ham and beans are tender.

4. Debone ham hocks and return cut-up meat to soup.

5. Taste before serving. Add salt if needed.

Tip:

If you want to reduce the amount of meat you eat, this dish is flavorful using only 1 ham hock.

Split Pea Soup

Judy Gascho, Woodburn, OR

Makes 3–4 servings

Prep. Time: 20 minutes & Cooking Time: 15 minutes & Recommended Instant Pot size: 6-qt.

4 cups chicken broth

4 sprigs thyme

4 oz. ham, diced (about ⅓ cup)

2 Tbsp. butter

2 stalks celery

2 carrots

I large leek

3 cloves garlic

I½ cups dried green split peas (about 12 oz.)

Salt and pepper to taste

1. Pour the broth into the inner pot of the Instant Pot and set to Sauté. Add the thyme, ham, and butter.

2. While the broth heats, chop the celery and cut the carrots into ½-inch-thick rounds. Halve the leek lengthwise and thinly slice and chop the garlic. Add the vegetables to the pot as you cut them. Rinse the split peas in a colander, discarding any small stones, then add to the pot.

3. Secure the lid, making sure the steam valve is in the sealing position. Set the cooker to Manual at high pressure for 15 minutes. When the time is up, carefully turn the steam valve to the venting position to release the pressure manually.

4. Turn off the Instant Pot. Remove the lid and stir the soup; discard the thyme sprigs.

5. Thin the soup with up to one cup water if needed (the soup will continue to thicken as it cools). Season with salt and pepper.

Potato Bacon Soup

Colleen Heatwole, Burton, MI

Makes 4–6 servings

Prep. Time: 30 minutes & Cooking Time: 5 minutes & Recommended Instant Pot size: 6-qt.

5 lb. potatoes, peeled and cubed

3 stalks of celery, diced into roughly ¼- to ½-inch pieces

1 large onion, chopped

1 clove garlic, minced

1 Tbsp. seasoning salt

½ tsp. black pepper

4 cups chicken broth

1 lb. bacon, fried crisp and rough chopped

1 cup half-and-half

1 cup milk, 2% or whole

Garnish (optional):

Sour cream

Shredded cheddar cheese

Diced green onion

Bacon pieces

Fresh herbs

1. Place potatoes in bottom of the Instant Pot inner pot.

2. Add celery, onion, garlic, seasoning salt, and pepper, then stir to combine.

3. Add chicken broth and bacon to pot and stir to combine.

4. Secure the lid and make sure vent is in the sealing position. Using Manual mode, select 5 minutes, high pressure.

5. Manually release the pressure when cooking time is up. Open pot and roughly mash potatoes, leaving some large chunks if desired.

6. Add half-and-half and milk.

7. Serve while still hot with desired assortment of garnishes.

Notes:

- I like this recipe because it requires no sautéing of onion, garlic, or celery but still tastes good.
- I have used a variety of potatoes for this recipe. We raise mostly Kennebec but also red potatoes. My spouse likes this recipe with either.

Shredded Pork Tortilla Soup

Hope Comerford, Clinton Township, MI

Makes 6–8 servings
Prep. Time: 10 minutes 🍂 Cooking Time: 8–10 hours 🍂 Ideal slow-cooker size: 5-qt.

3 large tomatoes, chopped

1 cup chopped red onion

1 jalapeño, seeded and minced

1 lb. pork loin

2 tsp. cumin

2 tsp. chili powder

2 tsp. onion powder

2 tsp. garlic powder

2 tsp. lime juice

8 cups chicken broth

Garnish (optional):

Fresh chopped cilantro

Tortilla chips

Avocado slices

Freshly grated Mexican cheese

1. In your crock, place the tomatoes, onion, and jalapeño.

2. Place the pork loin on top.

3. Add all the seasonings and lime juice, then pour in the chicken broth.

4. Cover and cook on Low for 8–10 hours.

5. Remove the pork and shred it between two forks. Place it back into the soup and stir.

6. Serve each bowl of soup with fresh chopped cilantro, tortilla chips, avocado slices, and freshly grated Mexican cheese, if desired . . . or any other garnishes you would like!

Tip:

If you don't have time for freshly chopped tomatoes, use a can of diced or chopped tomatoes.

Beef Soups

Beef Vegetable Soup

Anona M. Teel, Bangor, PA

Makes 6 servings
Prep. Time: 15 minutes & Cooking Time: 8–10 hours & Ideal slow-cooker size: 6½-qt.

1–1½-lb. soup bone
1 lb. stewing beef cubes
1½ qt. cold water
1 Tbsp. salt
¾ cup diced celery
¾ cup diced carrots
¾ cup diced potatoes
¾ cup diced onion
1 cup frozen mixed vegetables of your choice
16-oz. can diced tomatoes
⅛ tsp. pepper
1 Tbsp. chopped dried parsley

1. Put all ingredients in slow cooker.

2. Cover. Cook on Low 8–10 hours. Remove bone before serving.

Meatball and Pasta Soup

Michele Ruvola, Vestal, NY

Makes 4–5 servings

Prep. Time: 10 minutes & Cooking Time: 9 minutes & Recommended Instant Pot size: 6-qt.

1 cup diced carrots

½ cup diced celery

¾ cup diced onion

20–25 mini meatballs, frozen

1½ cups ditalini pasta

40 oz. beef broth

1 tsp. salt

½ tsp. black pepper

2 Tbsp. diced parsley

2 Tbsp. diced green onions

1. Place all ingredients except parsley and green onions in the inner pot of the Instant Pot and stir.

2. Secure the lid, make sure vent is set to sealing, then put on Manual function, set to high pressure, for 9 minutes.

3. Use quick release to release pressure, then stir.

4. Top with parsley and green onions.

Beef Goulash Vegetable Soup

SLOW COOKER

Betty Moore, Plano, IL

Makes 6 servings
Prep. Time: 20 minutes ❧ Cooking Time: 5–6 hours ❧ Ideal slow-cooker size: 4-qt.

1 lb. extra-lean ground beef
1 large onion, diced
2 ribs celery, chopped
8-oz. can tomato sauce
3 (14½-oz.) cans beef broth
10-oz. pkg. frozen green beans
1½ tsp. chili powder
1 tsp. paprika
½ tsp. black pepper
1½ cups flat wide noodles, cooked

1. Sauté ground beef, onion, and celery in nonstick skillet until meat is browned and vegetables are crisp-tender. Transfer to slow cooker.

2. Add tomato sauce, broth, green beans, chili powder, paprika, and black pepper. Mix together.

3. Cook on Low 5–6 hours.

4. Add noodles 15 minutes before serving.

Unstuffed Cabbage Soup

Colleen Heatwole, Burton, MI

Makes 4–6 servings
Prep. Time: 15 minutes   ⚬   Cooking Time: 10–20 minutes   ⚬   Recommended Instant Pot size: 6-qt.

2 Tbsp. coconut oil

1 lb. ground beef, turkey, or venison

1 medium onion, diced

2 cloves garlic, minced

1 small head cabbage, cored, chopped, cut into roughly 2-inch pieces.

6-oz. can tomato paste

32-oz. can diced tomatoes, with liquid

2 cups beef broth

1½ cups water

¾ cup white or brown rice

1–2 tsp. salt

½ tsp. black pepper

1 tsp. oregano

1 tsp. parsley

1. Melt coconut oil in the inner pot of the Instant Pot using Sauté function. Add ground meat. Stir frequently until meat loses color, about 2 minutes.

2. Add onion and garlic and continue to sauté for 2 more minutes, stirring frequently.

3. Add chopped cabbage.

4. On top of cabbage layer tomato paste, tomatoes with liquid, beef broth, water, rice, and spices.

5. Secure the lid and set vent to sealing. Using Manual setting, select 10 minutes if using white rice, 20 minutes if using brown rice.

6. When time is up, let the pressure release naturally for 10 minutes, then do a quick release.

Note:

I use home-canned tomatoes in this recipe and break them up slightly in the pot. This is the equivalent of 2 (15-oz.) cans of store-bought diced tomatoes.

Cabbage and Beef Soup

Colleen Heatwole, Burton, MI

Makes 6–8 servings
Prep. Time: 20 minutes ☘ Cooking Time: 6–8 hours ☘ Ideal slow-cooker size: 6-qt.

1 lb. extra-lean ground beef

28- or 32-oz. can tomatoes or 1 qt. home-canned tomatoes

¼ tsp. onion powder

1 tsp. garlic powder

¼ tsp. pepper

16-oz. can kidney beans, rinsed and drained

2 stalks celery, chopped

½ head cabbage, chopped

8 cups low-sodium beef stock

¼ cup water

Garnish:

Chopped fresh parsley

1. Brown beef in large skillet, then drain any drippings. Add tomatoes and chop coarsely. Transfer to slow cooker.

2. Add remaining ingredients except parsley.

3. Cover and cook 6–8 hours on Low.

4. Serve in bowls garnished with fresh parsley.

Variations:

Lean ground turkey may be used.
Black beans or small red beans may be substituted for the kidney beans.

Tip:

This soup freezes well.

Beef Barley Soup

SLOW COOKER

Michelle Showalter, Bridgewater, VA

Makes 10–12 servings
Prep. Time: 15 minutes   ♣   Cooking Time: 4–10 hours   ♣   Ideal slow-cooker size: 6-qt.

1 lb. extra-lean ground beef

1½ qt. water

1 qt. canned tomatoes, stewed, crushed, or whole

3 cups sliced carrots

1 cup diced celery

1 cup diced potatoes

1 cup diced onions

¾ cup quick-cooking barley

3 tsp. low-sodium beef bouillon granules, or 3 low-sodium beef bouillon cubes

2 tsp. kosher salt

¼ tsp. pepper

1. Brown ground beef in skillet. Stir frequently to break up clumps of meat. When meat is no longer pink, drain off drippings.

2. Place meat in cooker, along with all other ingredients. Mix together well.

3. Cover. Cook on Low 8–10 hours or on High 4–5 hours.

Variation:

You may use pearl barley instead of quick-cooking barley. Cook it in a saucepan according to package directions, and add halfway through soup's cooking time.

Beef Mushroom Barley Soup

Becky Frey, Lebanon, PA

Makes 8 servings

Prep. Time: 20 minutes & Cook Time: 25 minutes & Recommended Instant Pot size: 6-qt.

2 Tbsp. olive oil, *divided*

1 lb. boneless beef chuck, cubed

1 large onion, chopped

2 cloves garlic, crushed

1 lb. fresh mushrooms, sliced

1 celery stalk, sliced

2 carrots, sliced

½ tsp. dried thyme, *optional*

8 cups low-sodium beef stock

½ cup uncooked pearl barley

½ tsp. freshly ground pepper

3 Tbsp. chopped fresh parsley

1. Set the Instant Pot to the Sauté function and heat 1 Tbsp. of the olive oil in the inner pot.

2. Brown the beef, in batches if needed, and then remove and set aside.

3. Add the remaining Tbsp. of olive oil and sauté the onion, garlic, and mushrooms for 3 to 4 minutes.

4. Add the beef back in, as well as all the remaining ingredients, except for the parsley. Press Cancel.

5. Secure the lid and set the vent to sealing.

6. Manually set the cook time to 25 minutes on high pressure.

7. When the cook time is over, let the pressure release naturally for 15 minutes, then manually release the remaining pressure.

8. When the pin drops, remove the lid and stir. Serve each bowl topped with some fresh chopped parsley.

Hope's Taco Soup

Hope Comerford, Clinton Township, MI

Makes 4–6 servings
Prep. Time: 20 minutes 🌿 Cooking Time: 8 hours 🌿 Ideal slow-cooker size: 4-qt.

I lb. ground beef
I large onion, chopped
Salt and pepper to taste
I-oz. pkg. ranch dressing/seasoning mix
I pkg. taco seasoning
I tsp. cumin
I tsp. garlic powder
I cup pinto beans
15½-oz. can chili beans
I cup frozen whole kernel corn
2 (14½-oz.) cans diced tomatoes (chili flavor)
4 cups beef broth or stock

1. Brown ground beef with the onion, salt, and pepper.

2. Place the browned meat into the crock and add all the remaining ingredients. Stir.

3. Cover and cook on Low for 8 hours.

Serving suggestion:
Serve with sour cream, cheese, and tortilla chips.

Tip:
This recipe does great doubled.

Velveeta Cheese Soup

SLOW COOKER

Colleen Heatwole, Burton, MI

Makes 6–8 servings
Prep. Time: 20 minutes & Cooking Time: 4–6 hours & Ideal slow-cooker size: 6-qt.

1 lb. ground beef
1 medium onion, chopped finely
1 lb. Velveeta® cheese (can use store brand), cubed
15- or 15¼-oz. can corn, undrained
15-oz. can kidney beans, undrained
15-oz. can black beans, undrained
30- to 32-oz. canned tomatoes
2 Tbsp. dry taco seasoning mix

1. Brown beef with onion. Drain.

2. Combine all ingredients and add along with beef and onion to slow cooker.

3. Cover and cook on Low 4–6 hours.

Steak and Wild Rice Soup

Sally Holzem, Schofield, WI

Makes 6 servings

Prep. Time: 15 minutes   Cooking Time: 5 hours   Ideal slow-cooker size: 5-qt.

4 cups beef stock

3 cups cubed, cooked roast beef

4 oz. fresh mushrooms, sliced

½ cup chopped onion

¼ cup ketchup

2 tsp. apple cider vinegar

I tsp. brown sugar

I tsp. gluten-free Worcestershire sauce

⅛ tsp. ground mustard

I½ cups cooked wild rice

I cup frozen peas

1. Combine stock, beef, mushrooms, onion, ketchup, vinegar, sugar, Worcestershire sauce, and mustard in slow cooker.

2. Cook on Low 4 hours.

3. Add rice and peas. Cook an additional hour on Low.

Tip:

This is a great way to use up scraps of meat and broth left from a roast beef, and a nice way to transform leftover wild rice.

Seafood Soups

Crabmeat Soup

(Anonymous)

SLOW COOKER

Makes 8 servings

Prep. Time: 5 minutes ⚘ *Cooking Time: 5 hours* ⚘ *Ideal slow-cooker size: 3½-qt.*

2 (10¾-oz.) cans cream of tomato soup

2 (10½-oz.) cans split pea soup

4 cups milk

1 cup heavy cream

1–2 (6-oz.) cans crabmeat, drained

¼ cup sherry, *optional*

1. Pour soups into slow cooker. Add milk and stir to mix. Cover and cook on Low 4 hours or until hot.

2. Stir in cream and crabmeat. Continue to cook on Low 1 hour more or until heated through.

Hot & Sour Soup

SLOW COOKER

Judy Govotsos, Frederick, MD

Makes 4 servings
Prep. Time: 20 minutes   &   Cooking Time: 4½–6 hours   &   Ideal slow-cooker size: 3½-qt.

4 cups low-sodium chicken broth

8-oz. can sliced bamboo shoots, drained

1 carrot, julienned

8-oz. can water chestnuts, drained and sliced

3 Tbsp. quick-cooking tapioca

6-oz. can sliced mushrooms, drained

1 Tbsp. vinegar, or rice wine vinegar

1 Tbsp. light soy sauce

1 tsp. sugar

¼ tsp. black pepper

¼–½ tsp. red pepper flakes, according to your taste preference

8-oz. pkg. frozen, peeled, and deveined shrimp, *optional*

4 oz. firm tofu, drained and cubed

1 egg, beaten

1. Combine all ingredients, except shrimp, tofu, and egg in slow cooker.

2. Cover. Cook on Low 3¾–5 hours.

3. Add shrimp and tofu.

4. Cover. Cook 45–60 minutes.

5. Pour egg into the soup in a thin stream. Stir the soup gently until the egg forms fine shreds instead of clumps.

Meatless Soups

Creamy Tomato Soup

Susie Shenk Wenger, Lancaster, PA

Makes 4 servings
Prep. Time: 10–15 minutes   ♣   Cooking Time: 3–4 hours   ♣   Ideal slow-cooker size: 3-qt.

29-oz. can tomato sauce, or crushed tomatoes, or 1 qt. home-canned tomatoes, chopped

1 small onion, chopped

1–2 carrots, sliced thin

2 tsp. brown sugar

1 tsp. Italian seasoning

¼ tsp. salt

¼ tsp. pepper

1 tsp. freshly chopped parsley

½ tsp. Worcestershire sauce

1 cup heaving whipping cream

Croutons, preferably homemade

Freshly grated Parmesan cheese

1. Combine tomato sauce, onion, carrots, brown sugar, Italian seasoning, salt, pepper, parsley, and Worcestershire sauce in slow cooker.

2. Cover. Cook on Low 3–4 hours, or until vegetables are soft.

3. Cool soup a bit. Puree with immersion blender.

4. Add cream and blend lightly again.

5. Serve hot with croutons and Parmesan as garnish.

Tip:

This recipe can be easily doubled.

Fresh Tomato Soup

Rebecca Leichty, Harrisonburg, VA

Makes 6 servings
Prep. Time: 20–25 minutes ❧ *Cooking Time: 3–4 hours* ❧ *Ideal slow-cooker size: 3½- or 4-qt.*

5 cups ripe tomatoes, diced
(your choice about whether or not to
peel them)

1 Tbsp. tomato paste

4 cups salt-free vegetable broth

1 carrot, grated

1 onion, minced

1 Tbsp. minced garlic

1 tsp. dried basil

Pepper to taste

2 Tbsp. lemon juice

1 bay leaf

1. Combine all ingredients in a slow cooker.

2. Cook on Low for 3–4 hours. Stir once while cooking.

3. Remove bay leaf before serving.

French Onion Soup

Hope Comerford, Clinton Township, MI

Makes 6–8 servings
Prep. Time: 10 minutes & Cooking Time: 7–8 hours & Ideal slow-cooker size: 5-qt.

3–4 large sweet yellow onions,
sliced thinly

½ tsp. pepper

1 bay leaf

2 sprigs fresh thyme

7 cups low-sodium beef or
vegetable stock

1 cup dry white wine
(such as a chardonnay)

6–8 slices bread, crusts removed

4 oz. Gruyère cheese, sliced thinly

1. Place all of the onions into the crock and sprinkle them with the pepper. Add the bay leaf and sprigs of thyme.

2. Pour in the beef stock and wine.

3. Cover and cook on Low for 7–8 hours. Remove the thyme sprigs and bay leaf.

4. Serve each serving of soup in an oven-safe bowl and cover the soup with a slice of bread topped with cheese. Place it in the oven under the broiler for a few minutes, or until the cheese starts to bubble.

Cream of Pumpkin Soup

SLOW COOKER

Nanci Keatley, Salem, OR

Makes 4–6 servings

Prep. Time: 10–15 minutes ⚬ *Cooking Time: 3–4 hours* ⚬ *Ideal slow-cooker size: 4-qt.*

I Tbsp. butter, melted
I large onion, diced fine
32-oz. box vegetable stock
16-oz. can solid-pack pumpkin
I tsp. salt
¼ tsp. cinnamon
¼ tsp. freshly ground nutmeg
⅛ tsp. ginger
⅛ tsp. cloves
⅛ tsp. cardamom
¼ tsp. freshly ground pepper
1½ cups low-fat half-and-half
I cup heavy cream
Chopped chives

1. Mix butter and onion in slow cooker.

2. Add stock, pumpkin, salt, and other seasonings. Mix well.

3. Cover. Cook on Low 2–3 hours.

4. Add half-and-half and cream.

5. Cover. Cook on Low 1 hour, or until heated through.

6. Garnish individual serving bowls with chives.

Creamy Butternut Squash Soup

Hope Comerford, Clinton Township, MI

SLOW COOKER

Makes 4–6 servings

Prep. Time: 20 minutes ❧ *Cooking Time: 8 hours* ❧ *Ideal slow-cooker size: 3-qt.*

1½ lb. butternut squash, peeled and cut into 1-inch chunks

1 small onion, quartered

1 carrot, cut into 1-inch chunks

1 small sweet potato, cut into 1-inch chunks

¼ tsp. cinnamon

⅛ tsp. nutmeg

½ tsp. sugar

¼ tsp. salt

⅛ tsp. pepper

⅛ tsp. ginger

3 cups vegetable stock (or you can use chicken stock)

1 cup half-and-half

1. Place the butternut squash, onion, carrot, and sweet potato pieces into your crock.

2. Sprinkle the contents of the crock with the cinnamon, nutmeg, sugar, salt, pepper, and ginger. Pour the stock over the top.

3. Cover and cook on Low for 8 hours, or until the vegetables are soft.

4. Using an immersion blender, blend the soup until smooth.

5. Remove ¼ cup of the soup and mix it with 1 cup of half-and-half. Pour this into the crock and mix until well combined.

Creamy Potato Soup

Hope Comerford, Clinton Township, MI

Makes 6 servings
Prep. Time: 20 minutes ⚘ Cooking Time: 8–10 hours ⚘ Ideal slow-cooker size: 5-qt.

8–9 Idaho potatoes, chopped into
bite-sized pieces

4½ cups low-sodium vegetable broth

½ cup low-fat milk

1 medium onion, chopped

2–4 carrots, chopped

1–2 stalks celery, chopped

3 green onions, chopped

8-oz. block reduced-fat cream cheese,
chopped into cubes

¼ cup nonfat plain Greek yogurt

3 Tbsp. cornstarch

2 Tbsp. butter

2 tsp. garlic powder

1 tsp. onion powder

1½ tsp. pepper

1 tsp. salt

1. Place all ingredients into your crock and stir.

2. Cook on Low for 8–10 hours.

Serving suggestion:

Serve with fresh chopped chives or green onions on top and little bit of shredded cheese.

Tip:

Use an immersion blender to give your soup a smoother and creamier texture.

Easy Potato Soup

Yvonne Kauffman Boettger, Harrisonburg, VA

Makes 8 servings
Prep. Time: 10 minutes ⚸ *Cooking Time: 5 hours* ⚸ *Ideal slow-cooker size: 4- to 6-qt.*

3 cups vegetable broth

2-lb. bag frozen hash brown potatoes

1½ tsp. salt

¾ tsp. pepper

3 cups milk

3 cups shredded Monterey Jack or cheddar cheese

1. Place vegetable broth, potatoes, salt, and pepper in slow cooker.

2. Cover and cook on High 4 hours, or until potatoes are soft.

3. Leaving the broth and potatoes in the slow cooker, mash the potatoes lightly, leaving some larger chunks.

4. Add milk and cheese. Blend in thoroughly.

5. Cover and cook on High until cheese melts and soup is hot.

Broccoli Cheese Soup

Hope Comerford, Clinton Township, MI

Makes 6 servings
Prep. Time: 15 minutes   Cooking Time: 6–7 hours   Ideal slow-cooker size: 3-qt.

1 head broccoli, chopped into tiny pieces

1 onion, chopped finely

2 (12-oz.) cans evaporated milk

10¾-oz. can condensed cheddar cheese soup

3 cups water

4 vegetable boulllon cubes

1½ tsp. garlic powder

1 tsp. onion powder

½ tsp. seasoned salt

1 tsp. pepper

16-oz. block Velveeta® cheese, chopped into pieces

1. Place all ingredients into crock, except for the Velveeta cheese, and stir.

2. Cover and cook on Low for 6–7 hours.

3. About 5–10 minutes before eating, turn slow cooker to High and stir in Velveeta cheese until melted.

Cream of Broccoli Soup

Hope Comerford, Clinton Township, MI

Makes 4 servings
Prep. Time: 10 minutes 🌣 Cook Time: 5 minutes 🌣 Recommended Instant Pot size: 6-qt.

2 Tbsp. butter or margarine

1 medium onion, chopped

2 cloves garlic, chopped

1 lb. (about 5 cups) chopped fresh broccoli

4 cups chicken or vegetable stock

½ tsp. salt

¼ tsp. pepper

2 Tbsp. cornstarch

1 cup heavy cream, *divided*

½ cup shredded cheddar cheese

1. Set the Instant Pot to Sauté and melt the butter.

2. When the butter is melted, sauté the onion and garlic for 5 minutes.

3. Press Cancel and add the broccoli, stock, salt, and pepper.

4. Secure the lid and set the vent to sealing.

5. Manually set the cook time to 5 minutes on high pressure.

6. When the cook time is over, manually release the pressure.

7. When the pin drops, remove the lid and use a potato smasher to break up the broccoli a bit and thicken the soup.

8. In a small dish, mix the cornstarch with a bit of the heavy cream until smooth. Then, whisk the cornstarch/heavy cream with the remaining heavy cream and *slowly* whisk this mixture into the soup.

9. Serve each bowl with a sprinkle of shredded cheddar cheese and enjoy!

Creamy Wild Rice Mushroom Soup

Hope Comerford, Clinton Township, MI

Makes 4–6 servings

Prep. Time: 10 minutes ⚹ *Cook Time: 40 minutes* ⚹ *Recommended Instant Pot size: 6-qt.*

½ large onion, chopped

3 cloves garlic, chopped

3 celery stalks, chopped

3 carrots, chopped

8 oz. fresh baby bella mushrooms, sliced

1 cup wild rice

4 cups low-sodium chicken or vegetable stock

½ tsp. dried thyme

¼ tsp. pepper

1 cup fat-free half-and-half, heated

2 Tbsp. cornstarch

2 Tbsp. cold water

1. Place the onion, garlic, celery, carrots, mushrooms, wild rice, stock, thyme, and pepper in the inner pot of the Instant Pot and secure the lid. Make sure the vent is set to sealing.

2. Manually set the time for 30 minutes on high pressure.

3. When the cook time is over, manually release the pressure and remove the lid when the pin drops.

4. While the pressure is releasing, heat the half-and-half either in the microwave or on the stovetop.

5. Whisk together the cornstarch and cold water. Whisk this into the heated half-and-half.

6. Slowly whisk the half-and-half/cornstarch mixture into the soup in the Instant Pot. Serve and enjoy!

Cannellini Bean Soup

Hope Comerford, Clinton Township, MI

Makes 6–8 servings
Prep. Time: 10 minutes ⚶ Soaking Time: overnight (optional)
Cooking Time: 30 minutes ⚶ Recommended Instant Pot size: 6-qt.

2 Tbsp. extra-virgin olive oil

4 cloves garlic, sliced very thin

1 small onion, chopped

2 heads escarole, well washed and cut medium-fine (about 8 cups)

8-oz. bag dry cannellini beans, soaked overnight

8 cups low-sodium chicken or vegetable stock

3 basil leaves, chopped fine

Parmesan cheese shavings, *optional*

1. Set the Instant Pot to Sauté and heat the olive oil.

2. Sauté the garlic, onion, and escarole until the onion is translucent.

3. Hit the Cancel button on your Instant Pot and add the beans and stock.

4. Secure the lid and set the vent to sealing.

5. Manually set the time for 25 minutes on high pressure.

6. When the cooking time is over, let the pressure release naturally. Remove the lid when the pin drops and spoon into serving bowls.

7. Top each bowl with a sprinkle of the chopped basil leaves and a few Parmesan shavings (if using).

Tip:

If you do not remember to soak the beans overnight, or if you don't have time to soak them, simply cook the soup on high pressure for 51 minutes instead.

White Bean Soup

Esther H. Becker, Gordonville, PA

Makes 6 servings
Prep. Time: 5 minutes   ⚘   Soaking Time: overnight (optional)
Cooking Time: 9 minutes   ⚘   Recommended Instant Pot size: 6-qt.

8 oz. (about 1¼ cups) dried white beans

4 cups water

3 cups low-fat, low-sodium chicken or vegetable stock

1 tsp. grapeseed or olive oil

1 onion, diced

2 cups diced raw sweet potatoes (about 2 medium potatoes)

1 cup diced green bell pepper

¼ tsp. ground cloves

¼ tsp. black pepper

½ tsp. dried thyme

½ cup low-sugar ketchup

¼ cup molasses

1. In a pot of water, soak the beans overnight. Drain and rinse. Place drained beans in the inner pot of the Instant Pot.

2. Pour in the water, stock, grapeseed oil, onion, sweet potato, bell pepper, ground cloves, black pepper, and thyme.

3. Secure the lid and set the vent to sealing.

4. Manually set the cook time to 9 minutes at high pressure.

5. When the cooking time is over, allow the pressure to release naturally. When the pin drops, remove the lid.

6. Stir in the ketchup and molasses. Add more water if you would like your soup to be thinner.

Tips:

1. Adding the tsp. of oil to the pot keeps foam at a minimum to prevent clogging the vent.

2. If you don't want to soak the beans, or forget to soak the beans, simply set the cook time to 31 minutes on high pressure.

White Bean Fennel Soup

Janie Steele, Moore, OK

Makes 6 servings

Prep. Time: 20–30 minutes ⚜ *Cooking Time: 1–3 hours* ⚜ *Ideal slow-cooker size: 5-qt.*

1 Tbsp. olive, or canola, oil

1 large onion, chopped

1 small fennel bulb, sliced thin

5 cups fat-free chicken or
vegetable broth

15-oz. can white kidney, or cannellini,
beans, rinsed and drained

14½-oz. can diced tomatoes, undrained

1 tsp. dried thyme

¼ tsp. black pepper

1 bay leaf

3 cups chopped fresh spinach

1. Sauté onion and fennel in oil in skillet until brown.

2. Combine onion, fennel, broth, beans, tomatoes, thyme, pepper, and bay leaf.

3. Cook on Low 2–3 hours, or on High 1 hour, until fennel and onions are tender.

4. Remove bay leaf.

5. Add spinach about 10 minutes before serving.

Barley-Mushroom Soup

Janie Steele, Moore, OK

Makes 8 servings
Prep. Time: 25–30 minutes ⚜ *Cooking Time: 4–5 hours* ⚜ *Ideal slow-cooker size: 5-qt.*

6 cups fresh mushrooms, sliced

2 large onions, chopped

3 cloves garlic, minced

1 cup chopped celery

1 cup chopped carrots

5 cups water

¼ cup dry quick-cooking pearl barley

4 cups low-sodium beef or vegetable broth

4 tsp. Worcestershire sauce

1–1½ tsp. salt, *optional*

1½ tsp. dried basil

1½ tsp. dried parsley flakes

1 tsp. dill weed

1½ tsp. dried oregano

½ tsp. salt-free seasoning blend

½ tsp. dried thyme

½ tsp. garlic powder

1. Combine all ingredients in slow cooker.

2. Cook on Low 4–5 hours, or until vegetables and barley are done to your liking.

Barley Cabbage Soup

Betty K. Drescher, Quakertown, PA

Makes 8 servings
Prep. Time: 20 minutes ❧ Cooking Time: 4–10 hours ❧ Ideal slow-cooker size: 3½- or 4-qt.

¼ cup dry pearl barley

6 cups fat-free, low-sodium chicken, beef, or vegetable broth

1 cup chopped onions

3–4 cups finely chopped green cabbage

¼ cup chopped fresh parsley

½ tsp. celery salt

½ tsp. salt

⅛ tsp. black pepper

1 Tbsp. instant tapioca

1. Combine all ingredients in slow cooker.

2. Cover. Cook on Low 8–10 hours or on High 4–5 hours.

Cabbage Veggie Soup

SLOW COOKER

Judy Govotsos, Frederick, MD

Makes 8 servings

Prep. Time: 25 minutes 🍃 Cooking Time: 2¾–7 hours 🍃 Ideal slow-cooker size: 5-qt.

1 cup sliced carrots

1 cup diced onions

4 cloves garlic, chopped

6 cups low-sodium vegetable broth

3–4 cups shredded cabbage (or coleslaw mix ready-cut)

1 cup green beans, fresh, canned, or frozen and thawed

2 Tbsp. tomato paste

1–1½ tsp. dried basil

¼–½ tsp. dried oregano

½ tsp. salt

1 very small zucchini, diced

1 very small yellow squash, diced

1. Combine all ingredients in slow cooker, except zucchini and squash.

2. Cover. Cook on Low 5–6 hours or on high 2–3 hours.

3. Add zucchini and squash.

4. Cover. Cook on Low 45 minutes to 1 hour.

Vegetarian Split Pea Soup

Colleen Heatwole, Burton, MI

Makes 6 servings

Prep. Time: 30 minutes ⚜ *Cooking Time: 5–6 hours* ⚜ *Ideal slow-cooker size: 6-qt.*

1 lb. split peas, sorted and rinsed
2 qt. low-sodium vegetable broth
2 cups water
1 large onion, chopped
2 cloves garlic, minced
3 stalks celery, chopped
3 medium carrots, chopped finely
2 bay leaves
1 tsp. kosher salt
1 tsp. black pepper

1. Combine all ingredients and add to slow cooker.

2. Cover and cook on Low 5–6 hours. Remove bay leaves and serve.

Serving suggestion:

If creamy texture is desired, blend with immersion blender.

Tip:

If desired, add more salt after cooking, but note that this will increase sodium content.

Hearty Bean and Vegetable Soup

SLOW COOKER

Jewel Showalter, Landisville, PA

Makes 8–10 servings
Prep. Time: 20–25 minutes & Cooking Time: 6–8 hours & Ideal slow-cooker size: 5-qt.

2 medium onions, sliced

2 cloves garlic, minced

2 Tbsp. olive oil

8 cups low-sodium vegetable broth

1 small head cabbage, chopped

2 large red potatoes, chopped

2 cups chopped celery

2 cups chopped carrots

4 cups corn

2 tsp. dried basil

1 tsp. dried marjoram

¼ tsp. dried oregano

1 tsp. salt

½ tsp. pepper

2 (15-oz.) cans navy beans, rinsed and drained

1. Sauté onions and garlic in oil in skillet. Transfer to large slow cooker.

2. Add remaining ingredients. Mix well.

3. Cover. Cook on Low 6–8 hours.

Variation:

Add 2–3 cups cooked and cut-up chicken 30 minutes before serving if you wish.

All-Vegetable Soup

Jean Harris Robinson, Pemberton, NJ

Makes 8–10 servings
Prep. Time: 25 minutes ⚶ Cooking Time: 4–6 hours ⚶ Ideal slow-cooker size: 4-qt.

2 Tbsp. olive oil

1 large white onion (Vidalia preferred), diced

2 medium carrots, diced

2 cloves garlic, minced

20-oz. pkg. frozen cubed butternut squash, or 4 cups chopped fresh

2 cups finely chopped cabbage

1 cup chopped kale, packed

½ tsp. ground allspice

¼ tsp. ground ginger, or 1 Tbsp. finely grated fresh ginger

4 sprigs fresh thyme, or 1 tsp. dried thyme

1 tsp. salt, or to taste

14-oz. can diced tomatoes with juice

1 qt. no-salt vegetable broth

1. Combine all ingredients in cooker.

2. Cook on Low 4–6 hours until veggies are soft.

Serving suggestions:

Add a dollop of Greek yogurt to the top of each bowl. Place some hot cooked grains, such as brown rice or quinoa, in soup bowls before ladling in soup.

Tip:

Refrigerate for several days or freeze for later. It is a family pleaser. I like to prep the vegetables the night before. I often use frozen vegetables and sometimes add leftover green beans or broccoli at the last minute before serving.

Black Bean Soup with Fresh Salsa

Hope Comerford, Clinton Township, MI

INSTANT POT

Makes 6–8 servings
Prep. Time: 5 minutes ⚬ Soaking Time: overnight
Cooking Time: 70 minutes ⚬ Recommended Instant Pot size: 6-qt.

8 oz. dry black beans, soaked overnight

7 cups low-sodium chicken or vegetable stock

5 cloves garlic, minced

I Tbsp. chili powder

I¼ tsp. cumin

I½ tsp. oregano

I tsp. salt

I tsp. olive oil

3 Tbsp. fat-free sour cream, *optional*

Salsa Ingredients:

⅓ cup fresh cilantro, washed and stemmed

½ onion, coarsely chopped

Juice of ½ lime

¼ tsp. salt

1. Place the beans, stock, garlic, chili powder, cumin, oregano, salt, and olive oil into the inner pot of the Instant Pot.

2. Secure the lid and set the vent to sealing.

3. Manually set the cook time for 70 minutes on high pressure.

4. While the soup is cooking, puree the cilantro, onion, lime juice, and salt in a food processor until smooth. Place in a small bowl and keep refrigerated until serving time.

5. When the cooking time is over, let the pressure release naturally.

6. When the pin drops, remove the lid and scoop out about 1 cup of cooked beans with a slotted spoon and place in a bowl. Using an immersion blender, puree the beans then stir them back into the pot.

7. Spoon soup into serving bowls and serve with a bit of optional sour cream and fresh salsa on top.

Tip:

Do not skip the olive oil. The oil in the pot keeps the foam from the cooking beans at a minimum to help prevent clogging the vent during cooking. You may replace the olive oil with canola or grapeseed oil instead if you wish.

Mediterranean Lentil Soup

INSTANT POT

Marcia S. Myer, Manheim, PA

Makes 6 servings
Prep. Time: 10 minutes & Cooking Time: 18 minutes & Recommended Instant Pot size: 6-qt.

2 Tbsp. olive oil

2 large onions, chopped

1 carrot, chopped

1 cup uncooked lentils

½ tsp. dried thyme

½ tsp. dried marjoram

3 cups low-sodium chicken stock or vegetable stock

14½-oz. can diced no-salt-added tomatoes

¼ cup chopped fresh parsley

¼ cup sherry, *optional*

⅔ cup grated low-fat cheese, *optional*

1. Set the Instant Pot to the Sauté function, then heat up the olive oil.

2. Sauté the onions and carrot until the onions are translucent, about 5 minutes.

3. Press the Cancel button, then add the lentils, thyme, marjoram, stock, and canned tomatoes.

4. Secure the lid and set the vent to sealing.

5. Manually set the cook time to 18 minutes at high pressure.

6. When the cooking time is over, manually release the pressure.

7. When the pin drops, stir in the parsley and sherry (if using).

8. When serving, add a sprinkle of grated low-fat cheese if you wish.

Minestrone

Bernita Boyts, Shawnee Mission, KS

Makes 8–10 servings
Prep. Time: 15 minutes ☙ Cooking Time: 4–9 hours ☙ Ideal slow-cooker size: 3½- to 4-qt.

1 large onion, chopped

4 carrots, sliced

3 stalks celery, sliced

2 cloves garlic, minced

1 Tbsp. olive oil

6-oz. can tomato paste

2 cups low-sodium chicken, beef, or vegetable broth

24-oz. can pinto beans, rinsed and drained

10-oz. pkg. frozen green beans

2–3 cups chopped cabbage

1 medium zucchini, sliced

8 cups water

2 Tbsp. parsley

2 Tbsp. Italian seasoning

1 tsp. sea salt, or more to taste

½ tsp. pepper

¾ cup dry acini di pepe (small round pasta)

Grated Parmesan or Asiago cheese, *optional*

1. Sauté onion, carrots, celery, and garlic in oil in skillet until tender. Add to slow cooker.

2. Combine all other ingredients, except pasta and cheese, in slow cooker.

3. Cover. Cook 4–5 hours on High or 8–9 hours on Low.

4. Add pasta 1 hour before cooking is complete.

5. Top individual servings with cheese, if desired.

Minestra Di Ceci

SLOW COOKER

(Anonymous)

Makes 4–6 servings
Prep. Time: 25 minutes ⚬ Soaking Time: 8 hours–overnight
Cooking Time: 5 ½–6 hours ⚬ Ideal slow-cooker size: 4-qt.

1 lb. dry chickpeas

1 sprig fresh rosemary

10 leaves fresh sage

2 Tbsp. salt

1–2 large cloves garlic, minced

Olive oil

1 cup uncooked small pasta, your choice of shape, or uncooked penne

Garnish:

Rosemary sprigs

1. Place washed chickpeas in slow cooker. Cover with water. Stir in rosemary, sage, and salt. Soak 8 hours, or overnight.

2. Drain water and remove herbs. Refill slow cooker with peas and fresh water to 1 inch above peas. Cover and cook on Low for 5 hours.

3. After 5 hours, puree half of peas, along with several cups of broth from cooker, in blender. Return puree to slow cooker.

4. Sauté garlic in olive oil in skillet. Add to slow cooker.

5. Boil pasta in saucepan until al dente, about 5 minutes. Drain. Add to beans. Cover and cook on High 30 to 60 minutes, or until pasta is tender. Garnish with rosemary sprigs.

Enchilada Soup

Melissa Paskvan, Novi, MI

Makes 6–8 servings
Prep. Time: 5 minutes & Cooking Time: 6–8 hours & Ideal slow-cooker size: 6-qt.

14½-oz. can diced tomatoes with green chilies or chipotle

12-oz. jar enchilada sauce

4 cups vegetable broth

1 small onion, chopped

3 cups sliced tricolor bell peppers

10-oz. pkg. frozen corn

1 cup water

½ cup uncooked quinoa

1. Add all ingredients to slow cooker.

2. Cover and cook on Low for 6–8 hours.

Egg Drop Soup

Shirley Unternahrer Hinh, Wayland, IA

Makes 8 servings
Prep. Time: 30 minutes   ♣   Cooking Time: 1 hour   ♣   Ideal slow-cooker size: 3½-qt.

2 (14½-oz.) cans fat-free, low-sodium vegetable broth

1 qt. water

2 Tbsp. fish sauce

¼ tsp. salt

4 Tbsp. cornstarch

1 cup cold water

2 eggs, beaten

1 chopped green onion

¼ tsp. black pepper

1. Combine broth and water in large saucepan.

2. Add fish sauce and salt. Bring to boil.

3. Mix cornstarch into cold water until smooth. Add to soup. Bring to boil while stirring. Remove from heat.

4. Pour beaten eggs into thickened broth, but do not stir. Instead, pull fork through soup with 2 strokes.

5. Transfer to slow cooker. Add green onions and pepper and pull through soup with fork.

6. Cover. Cook on Low 1 hour. Keep warm in cooker.

Serving suggestion:
Eat plain or with rice.

Stews

Chicken Stews

Chicken Chili Pepper Stew

Susan Kasting, Jenks, OK

Makes 4 servings
Prep. Time: 5 minutes ⚜ *Cooking Time: 8 minutes* ⚜ *Recommended Instant Pot size: 6-qt.*

14½-oz. can low-sodium chicken stock

1 lb. boneless, skinless chicken breasts

4 cloves garlic, minced

1–2 jalapeño peppers, seeded and diced

1 medium red bell pepper, diced

1 medium carrot, sliced

15-oz. can corn, drained

1 tsp. cumin

2 Tbsp. chopped cilantro

1. Place all the ingredients, except the chopped cilantro, into the inner pot of the Instant Pot and secure the lid. Set the vent to sealing.

2. Manually set the cook time for 8 minutes on high pressure.

3. When the cooking time is over, let the pressure release naturally for 5 minutes, then manually release the pressure.

4. When the pin drops, remove the lid, remove the chicken, shred between two forks, then replace back in the inner pot. Stir.

5. Serve each bowl of stew with a sprinkling of chopped cilantro.

Chili Chicken Stew with Rice

Jenny R. Unternahrer, Wayland, IA

Makes 4–5 servings
Prep. Time: 30 minutes & *Cooking Time: 2½–5 hours* & *Ideal slow-cooker size: 2½-qt.*

1½ lb. chicken tenders*

½ small onion, diced

15-oz. can black beans, drained (not rinsed)

14½-oz. can petite diced tomatoes, undrained

1 cup whole corn, drained if needed (thawed if frozen)

2 tsp. chili powder

½ tsp. cumin

2–4 dashes cayenne pepper

1½ tsp. salt

2 cups cooked brown rice

Sour cream to taste

Shredded Mexican blend cheese to taste

1. Add all the ingredients, except brown rice, sour cream, and shredded cheese, to crock.

2. Mix. Cover and cook on High for 2½ hours or Low for 5 hours.

3. Shred chicken; stir to incorporate.

4. Serve over brown rice and add desired amount of sour cream and shredded Mexican blend cheese.

---

* You can try whole boneless, skinless chicken breasts, but allow more time to cook.

Lentil Barley Stew with Chicken

Ilene Bontrager, Arlington, KS

Makes 4 servings

Prep. Time: 8–11 minutes   ⚜   Cooking Time: 18 minutes   ⚜   Recommended Instant Pot size: 6-qt.

2 Tbsp. olive oil

½ onion, chopped

1 small celery rib, sliced thin

1 carrot, cut in fine dice

½ lb. boneless, skinless chicken breast, chopped

⅓ cup uncooked lentils, rinsed

⅓ cup uncooked green split peas

⅓ cup uncooked pearl barley

¼ tsp. pepper

6 cups low-sodium chicken stock

1. Set the Instant Pot to Sauté and heat the olive oil.

2. Sauté the onion, celery, and carrot for about 3 minutes, then add the chopped chicken. Continue cooking an additional 5 to 8 minutes or until the chicken is browned.

3. Press Cancel and add the lentils, split peas, pearl barley, pepper, and chicken stock.

4. Secure the lid and set the vent to sealing.

5. Manually set the cook time to 18 minutes on high pressure.

6. When the cooking time is over, let the pressure release naturally.

Very Shroomy Chicken Stew

Carolyn Spohn, Shawnee, KS

Makes 4–6 servings
Prep. Time: 15 minutes & Cooking Time: 4–6 hours & Ideal slow-cooker size: 5-qt.

1 large boneless chicken breast cut into 1-inch cubes
10¾-oz. can cream of chicken soup
10¾-oz. can cream of mushroom soup
1 cup sliced mushrooms
1 cup frozen mixed vegetables
2 Tbsp. dried minced onion
2 tsp. fresh minced garlic
1–2 tsp. dried rosemary leaves
1 tsp. dried oregano leaves

1. Place all ingredients in slow cooker; stir to mix.

2. Cover and cook on Low 4–6 hours.

Serving suggestion:
Serve over noodles or rice.

Turkey Stews

Ground Turkey Stew

INSTANT POT

Carol Eveleth, Cheyenne, WY

Makes 4–6 servings

Prep. Time: 5 minutes & Cooking Time: 25 minutes & Recommended Instant Pot size: 6-qt.

1 Tbsp. oil
1 onion, chopped
1 lb. ground turkey
½ tsp. garlic powder
1 tsp. chili powder
¾ tsp. cumin
2 tsp. coriander
1 tsp. dried oregano
½ tsp. salt
1 green pepper, chopped
1 red pepper, chopped
1 tomato, chopped
1½ cups tomato sauce
1 Tbsp. soy sauce
1 cup water
2 handfuls cilantro, chopped
15-oz. can black beans

Serving suggestion:

You can serve this with pasta—add pasta into a bowl and add cheddar cheese on top.

Note:

This also works well with ground beef.

1. Press the Sauté function on the control panel of the Instant Pot.

2. Add the oil to the inner pot and let it get hot. Add onion, season with salt, and sauté for a few minutes, or until light golden.

3. Add ground turkey. Break the ground meat using a wooden spoon to avoid formation of lumps. Sauté for a few minutes, until the pink color has faded.

4. Add garlic powder, chili powder, cumin, coriander, dried oregano, and salt. Combine well. Add green pepper, red pepper, and chopped tomato. Combine well.

5. Add tomato sauce, soy sauce, and water; combine well.

6. Close and secure the lid. Click on the Cancel key to cancel the Sauté mode. Make sure the pressure release valve on the lid is in the sealing position.

7. Click on Manual function first and then select high pressure. Click the + button and set the time to 15 minutes.

8. You can either have the steam release naturally (it will take around 20 minutes) or, after 10 minutes, turn the pressure release valve on the lid to venting and release steam. Be careful as the steam is very hot. After the pressure has released completely, open the lid.

9. If the stew is watery, turn on the Sauté function and let it cook for a few more minutes with the lid off.

10. Add cilantro and can of black beans, combine well, and let cook for a few minutes.

Zucchini Stew

Colleen Heatwole, Burton, MI

Makes 6 servings
Prep. Time: 30 minutes ⚘ *Cooking Time: 4–6 hours* ⚘ *Ideal slow-cooker size: 6-qt.*

I lb. Italian turkey sausage, sliced

2 stalks celery, diced

2 medium green bell peppers, diced

I medium onion, chopped

2 (28-oz.) cans diced tomatoes

2 lb. zucchini, cut into ½-inch slices

2 cloves garlic, minced

I tsp. sugar

I tsp. dried oregano

I tsp. Italian seasoning

I tsp. sea salt, *optional* (taste first)

6 Tbsp. grated Parmesan cheese, *optional*

1. Brown sausage in hot skillet until brown and crumbly, about 5–7 minutes. Drain and discard grease.

2. Mix celery, bell peppers, and onion into cooked sausage and cook and stir until they are softened, 10–12 minutes. Add sausage mixture to slow cooker.

3. Combine remaining ingredients, except Parmesan cheese, and add to slow cooker.

4. Cook on Low 4–6 hours. Garnish each serving with 1 Tbsp. Parmesan cheese if desired.

Turkey Sausage Stew

Sheridy Steele, Ardmore, OK

Makes 6 servings
Prep. Time: 25–30 minutes ⚬ *Cooking Time: 4–6 hours* ⚬ *Ideal slow-cooker size: 3½- or 4-qt.*

½ lb. turkey sausage, removed from casing

1 large onion, chopped

2 cloves garlic, minced

¾ cup chopped carrots

1 fennel bulb, chopped

½ cup chopped celery

10¾-oz. can reduced-sodium chicken broth

3 medium tomatoes, peeled, seeded, and chopped

1 tsp. dried basil

1 tsp. dried oregano

¼ tsp. salt

15-oz. can navy beans, rinsed and drained

1 cup uncooked shell pasta

½ cup low-fat Parmesan cheese

1. In nonstick skillet, brown turkey sausage, onion, and garlic. Drain well.

2. Combine all ingredients except pasta and cheese in slow cooker.

3. Cook on Low 4–6 hours.

4. One hour before end of cooking time, stir in pasta.

5. Sprinkle with cheese to serve.

Pork Stews

Quick Sausage Stew

Beverly Hummel, Fleetwood, PA

Makes 10 servings
Prep. Time: 20 minutes ⚬ Cooking Time: 4–5 hours ⚬ Ideal slow-cooker size: 7-qt.

2 Tbsp. beef bouillon
2 cups water
I lb. fresh Italian sausage, sliced thin
½ cup chopped onion
½ cup chopped bell pepper
I-lb. bag frozen carrots
I-lb. bag frozen green beans
4 medium potatoes, cubed
24-oz. can spaghetti sauce
Salt and pepper to taste
I Tbsp. Worcestershire sauce

1. Dissolve beef bouillon in the 2 cups water.

2. Brown sausage in skillet. Transfer to slow cooker.

3. Pour in bouillon/water and rest of ingredients.

4. Cover and cook on Low for 4–5 hours.

Tip:

This is a hearty soup, a great way to feed a large group. You may substitute ground beef for the sausage.

Easy Southern Brunswick Stew

SLOW COOKER

(Anonymous)

Makes 10–12 servings

Prep. Time:15 minutes ⚜ *Cooking Time: scant 9 hours* ⚜ *Ideal slow-cooker size: 4-qt.*

2–3 lb. pork butt

17-oz. can white corn

14-oz. bottle ketchup

2 cups diced cooked potatoes

10-oz. pkg. frozen peas

2 (10¾-oz.) cans tomato soup

Hot sauce to taste

Salt and pepper to taste

1. Place pork in slow cooker.

2. Cover and cook on High 1 hour. Turn temperature to Low and continue cooking 5 to 7 hours more. Remove meat from bone and shred.

3. Combine pork and remaining ingredients in slow cooker.

4. Cover. Bring to boil on High. Turn temperature to Low and simmer 30 minutes more.

Chet's Trucker Stew

Janice Muller, Derwood, MD

Makes 10 servings
Prep. Time: 30 minutes ⚬ Cooking Time: 3–4 hours ⚬ Ideal slow-cooker size: 5-qt.

1 lb. cooked Jimmy Dean's® Pork Sausage Links, drained and crumbled

1 can wax beans, drained

1 can lima beans, drained

1 lb. cooked ground beef or turkey, drained

1 cup ketchup

27-oz. can pork & beans with liquid

1 cup brown sugar

1 can light kidney beans with liquid

1 can dark kidney beans with liquid

1 Tbsp. Gulden's Spicy® Brown Mustard

1. Combine all ingredients in slow cooker.

2. Cover and cook on High for 3–4 hours.

Serving suggestion:

This pairs well with cornbread or a loaf of warm Italian bread.

Sausage and Black Bean Stew

John D. Allen, Rye, CO

Makes 6 servings

Prep. Time: 20 minutes ☙ Cooking Time: 5½–7½ hours ☙ Ideal slow-cooker size: 6-qt.

3 (15-oz.) cans black beans, rinsed and drained

14½-oz. can fat-free, reduced-sodium chicken broth

1 cup sliced celery

2 (4-oz.) cans green chilies, chopped

3 cloves garlic, minced

1½ tsp. dried oregano

¾ tsp. ground coriander

½ tsp. ground cumin

¼ tsp. ground red pepper (not cayenne)

1-lb. link pork sausage, thinly sliced and cooked

1. Combine all ingredients in slow cooker except sausage.

2. Cover. Cook on Low 5–7 hours.

3. Remove 1½ cups of bean mixture and purée in blender. Return to slow cooker.

4. Add sliced sausage.

5. Cover. Cook on Low 30 minutes.

Cider and Pork Stew

Veronica Sabo, Shelton, CT

Makes 5 servings
Prep. Time: 15 minutes ⚬ Cooking Time: 7–9 hours ⚬ Ideal slow-cooker size: 3½-qt.

2 medium (about 1¼ lb.) sweet potatoes, peeled if you wish, and cut into ¾-inch pieces

3 small carrots, peeled and cut into ½-inch-thick slices

1 cup chopped onions

1–2-lb. boneless pork shoulder, cut into 1-inch cubes

1 large Granny Smith apple, peeled, cored, and coarsely chopped

¼ cup flour

¾ tsp. salt

½ tsp. dried sage

½ tsp. thyme

½ tsp. pepper

1 cup apple cider

1. Layer sweet potatoes, carrots, onions, pork, and apple in slow cooker.

2. Combine flour, salt, sage, thyme, and pepper in medium bowl.

3. Add cider to flour mixture. Stir until smooth.

4. Pour cider mixture over meat and vegetables in slow cooker.

5. Cover. Cook on Low 7–9 hours, or until meat and vegetables are tender.

Creamy Pork Stew

Betty Moore, Plano, IL

Makes 8 servings
Prep. Time: 25–30 minutes ⚘ *Cooking Time: 6–8 hours* ⚘ *Ideal slow-cooker size: 5-qt.*

2 lb. ground pork

2 (10¾-oz.) cans cream of
mushroom soup

2 (14½-oz.) cans green beans with
liquid

4 potatoes, diced

4 carrots, chopped

2 small onions, diced

2 (10¾-oz.) cans condensed vegetarian
vegetable soup

2 soup cans water

3 ribs celery, chopped

½ tsp. salt

¼ tsp. black pepper

¼ tsp. garlic powder

½ tsp. dried marjoram

1. Brown ground pork in a nonstick skillet.

2. Combine all ingredients in slow cooker.

3. Cook on Low 6–8 hours.

Variations:

1. Add a can of diced tomatoes to Step 2 if you wish.
2. This recipe goes well with homemade bread.

Italian Shredded Pork Stew

Emily Fox, Bernville, PA

Makes 6–8 servings
Prep. Time: 20 minutes & Cooking Time: 8–10 hours & Ideal slow-cooker size: 5-qt.

2 medium sweet potatoes, peeled and cubed

2 cups chopped fresh kale

1 large onion, chopped

3 cloves garlic, minced

2½–3½ lb. boneless pork shoulder butt roast

14-oz. can white kidney or cannellini beans, drained

1½ tsp. Italian seasoning

½ tsp. salt

½ tsp. pepper

3 (14½-oz.) cans chicken broth

Sour cream, *optional*

1. Place first four ingredients in slow cooker.

2. Place roast on vegetables.

3. Add beans and seasonings.

4. Pour the broth over top.

5. Cover and cook on Low 8–10 hours or until meat is tender.

6. Remove meat. Skim fat from cooking juices if desired. Shred pork with two forks and return to cooker. Heat through.

7. Garnish with sour cream if desired.

Ham and Bean Stew

Sharon Wantland, Menomonee Falls, WI

Makes 4–6 servings
Prep. Time: 15 minutes ⚭ Cooking Time: 5–7 hours ⚭ Ideal slow-cooker size: 3-qt.

2 (16-oz.) cans baked beans

2 medium potatoes, peeled and cubed

2 cups cubed ham

2 ribs celery, chopped

1 onion, chopped

½ cup water

1 Tbsp. cider vinegar

1 tsp. salt

⅛ tsp. pepper

1. In a slow cooker, combine all ingredients. Mix well.

2. Cover and cook on Low for 5–7 hours, or until the potatoes are tender.

Beef & Lamb Stews

Slow-Cooker Beef Stew

Becky Fixel, Grosse Pointe Farms, MI

Makes 8–10 servings

Prep. Time: 30 minutes ⚜ *Cooking Time: 6 hours* ⚜ *Ideal slow-cooker size: 3-qt.*

2 lb. stewing beef, cubed

¼ cup white rice flour

1½ tsp. salt

½ tsp. black pepper

32 oz. beef broth

1 onion, diced

1 tsp. Worcestershire sauce

1 bay leaf

1 tsp. paprika

4 carrots, sliced

3 potatoes, sliced thinly

1 stalk celery, sliced

1. Place the meat in crock.

2. Mix the flour, salt, and pepper. Pour over the meat and mix well. Make sure to cover the meat with flour.

3. Add broth to the crock and stir well.

4. Add remaining ingredients and stir to mix well.

5. Cook on High for at least 5 hours, then on Low for 1 hour. Remove bay leaf and serve.

Instantly Good Beef Stew

Hope Comerford, Clinton Township, MI

Makes 6 servings
Prep. Time: 20 minutes ☙ Cook Time: 35 minutes ☙ Recommended Instant Pot size: 6-qt.

3 Tbsp. olive oil, *divided*

2 lb. stewing beef, cubed

2 cloves garlic, minced

1 large onion, chopped

3 ribs celery, sliced

3 large potatoes, cubed

2–3 carrots, sliced

8-oz. can no-salt-added tomato sauce

10-oz. can low-sodium beef broth

2 tsp. Worcestershire sauce

¼ tsp. pepper

1 bay leaf

1. Set the Instant Pot to the Sauté function, then add 1 Tbsp. of the oil. Add ⅓ of the beef cubes and brown and sear all sides. Repeat this process twice more with the remaining oil and beef cubes. Set the beef aside.

2. Place the garlic, onion, and celery into the pot and sauté for a few minutes. Press Cancel.

3. Add the beef back in as well as all the remaining ingredients.

4. Secure the lid and make sure the vent is set to sealing. Choose Manual for 35 minutes.

5. When the cook time is over, let the pressure release naturally for 15 minutes, then release any remaining pressure manually.

6. Remove the lid, remove the bay leaf, then serve.

Note:

If you want the stew to be a bit thicker, remove some of the potatoes, mash, then stir them back through the stew.

Tuscan Beef Stew

Orpha Herr, Andover, NY

Makes 12 servings
Prep. Time: 20 minutes ⚙ Cooking Time: 8–9⅓ hours ⚙ Ideal slow-cooker size: 6-qt.

10¾-oz. can tomato soup

1½ cups beef broth

½ cup burgundy wine or other red wine

1 tsp. Italian herb seasoning

½ tsp. garlic powder

14½-oz. can diced Italian-style tomatoes, undrained

½ cup diced onion

3 large carrots, cut into 1-inch pieces

2 lb. stewing beef, cut into 1-inch pieces

2 (16-oz.) cans cannellini beans, rinsed and drained

1. Stir soup, broth, wine, Italian seasoning, garlic powder, tomatoes, onion, carrots, and beef into slow cooker.

2. Cover and cook on Low 8–9 hours or until vegetables are tender-crisp.

3. Stir in beans. Turn to High until heated through, 10–20 minutes more.

Moroccan Beef Stew

Joyce Cox, Port Angeles, WA

Makes 4–6 servings

Prep. Time: 30 minutes ⚹ Cooking Time: 8–10 hours ⚹ Ideal slow-cooker size: 4-qt.

3 Tbsp. olive oil, *divided*

2 cups thinly sliced onion

5 cloves garlic, minced

2-lb. beef chuck roast, cut into 2-inch cubes, seasoned with salt and pepper

15-oz. can diced tomatoes with juice

1 cup low-sodium beef broth

1 Tbsp. honey

2 tsp. ground cumin

2 tsp. ground coriander

1 tsp. ground ginger

1 tsp. ground turmeric

1 cinnamon stick

1 bay leaf

Black pepper to taste

1 cup pitted, chopped prunes

1. Heat 1½ Tbsp. olive oil in large frying pan and sauté onions until golden brown. Add garlic and cook 1 more minute. Transfer to slow cooker.

2. Heat remaining 1½ Tbsp. oil in pan. Sear beef cubes on all sides. Transfer to slow cooker.

3. Add rest of ingredients to slow cooker. Stir well.

4. Cover and cook on Low for 8–10 hours. Remove cinnamon stick and bay leaf before serving.

Serving suggestion:
Serve over brown rice or quinoa.

Irish Stew

Rebecca Leichty, Harrisonburg, VA

Makes 8 servings
Prep. Time: 20 minutes ♣ Cooking Time: 5–6 hours ♣ Ideal slow-cooker size: 4- or 5-qt.

2 lb. boneless lamb, cubed

1½ tsp. salt

¼ tsp. black pepper

2 medium-sized carrots, sliced

1 large onion, diced

3 medium-sized potatoes, diced

1 bay leaf

2 cups water

¼ cup dry small pearl tapioca

1 can small, tender peas

1. Grease slow cooker with fat-free cooking spray.

2. Place cubed lamb in bottom of slow cooker. Season with salt and pepper.

3. Add carrots, onion, potatoes, and bay leaf.

4. Stir in water and tapioca.

5. Cover and cook on High 1 hour. Turn down to Low and cook 4–5 hours.

6. Add peas for last 30 minutes of cooking.

7. Remove bay leaf before serving.

Cider Beef Stew

Jean Turner, Williams Lake, BC

Makes 8 servings
Prep. Time: 30 minutes ♣ Cooking Time: 8–10¼ hours ♣ Ideal slow-cooker size: 3-qt.

2 lb. stewing beef, cut into 1-inch cubes
6 Tbsp. flour, *divided*
2 tsp. salt
¼ tsp. pepper
¼ tsp. dried thyme
3 Tbsp. cooking oil
4 potatoes, peeled and quartered
4 carrots, quartered
2 onions, sliced
1 rib celery, sliced
1 apple, chopped
2 cups apple cider or apple juice
1–2 Tbsp. vinegar
½ cup cold water

1. Stir together beef, 3 Tbsp. flour, salt, pepper, and thyme. Brown coated beef in oil in skillet. Do in two batches if necessary to avoid crowding the meat.

2. Place vegetables and apple in slow cooker. Place browned meat cubes on top.

3. Pour apple cider and vinegar over everything.

4. Cover and cook on Low for 8–10 hours.

5. Turn slow cooker to High. Blend cold water with remaining 3 Tbsp. flour. Stir into hot stew.

6. Cover and cook on High for 15 minutes, or until thickened.

Serving suggestion:
A side salad is all that is needed for a complete meal.

Pirate Stew

Nancy Graves, Manhattan, KS

Makes 4–6 servings
Prep. Time: 15 minutes   ♣   Cooking Time: 6 hours   ♣   Ideal slow-cooker size: 4-qt.

¾ cup sliced onion

1 lb. ground beef

¼ cup uncooked, long-grain rice

3 cups diced raw potatoes

1 cup diced celery

2 cups canned kidney beans, drained

1 tsp. salt

⅛ tsp. pepper

¼ tsp. chili powder

¼ tsp. Worcestershire sauce

1 cup tomato sauce

½ cup water

1. Brown onions and ground beef in skillet. Drain.

2. Layer ingredients in slow cooker in order given.

3. Cover. Cook on Low 6 hours, or until potatoes and rice are cooked.

Campfire Stew

Sharon Wantland, Menomonee Falls, WI

Makes 4 servings
Prep. Time: 15 minutes ⚖ *Cooking Time: 2–3 hours* ⚖ *Ideal slow-cooker size: 2-qt.*

1 lb. ground beef
1 medium onion, chopped
½ green pepper, chopped
Salt and pepper to taste
2 cans vegetable soup,
   your favorite variety

1. Brown ground beef with onions and green pepper in a nonstick skillet, stirring until crumbly. Drain.

2. Combine all ingredients in slow cooker.

3. Cover and cook on Low 2–3 hours.

Meme's Meatball Stew

Maxine Phaneuf, Washington, MI

Makes 6–8 servings
Prep. Time: 10 minutes ❧ Cook Time: 15 minutes ❧ Recommended Instant Pot size: 6-qt.

Meatballs:

1½ lb. lean ground beef

1 pkg. onion soup mix

¾ cup Italian bread crumbs

1 egg

Stew:

7 cups water

11¾-oz. can condensed tomato soup

2½ carrots, peeled and chopped

2 potatoes, peeled and chopped

2 big handfuls of fresh green beans, chopped

1 medium onion, chopped

1–2 tsp. salt

½ tsp. pepper

2 tsp. onion powder

2 tsp. garlic powder

1. In a medium bowl, mix the meatball ingredients and form into golf ball–sized meatballs.

2. In the inner pot of the Instant Pot, add the stew ingredients. Carefully drop in the meatballs.

3. Secure the lid and set the vent to sealing. Manually set the cook time for 15 minutes on high pressure.

4. When the cook time is over, let the pressure release naturally for 10 minutes, then manually release the remaining pressure.

Serving suggestion:

Serve each bowl with grated Parmesan cheese and a side of crusty Italian bread with butter.

Note:

You can use tomato sauce in place of the condensed tomato soup.

Meatless Stews

Veggie Stew

(Anonymous)

Makes 10–15 servings
Prep. Time: 20 minutes ⚘ Cooking Time: 9–11 hours ⚘ Ideal slow-cooker size: 8-qt.

5–6 potatoes, diced

3 carrots, diced

1 onion, chopped

½ cup chopped celery

2 cups canned diced or stewed tomatoes

3 vegetable bouillon cubes dissolved in 3 cups water

1½ tsp. dried thyme

½ tsp. dried parsley

½ cup brown rice, uncooked

1 lb. frozen green beans

1 lb. frozen corn

15-oz. can butter beans

46-oz. can vegetable juice (we used V8®)

1. Combine potatoes and next 8 ingredients in 8-qt. slow cooker or two medium-size slow cookers.

2. Cover and cook on High 2 hours. Puree one cup of mixture, then stir into slow cooker to thicken soup.

3. Stir in beans and remaining ingredients.

4. Cover and cook on High 1 hour and then on Low 6 to 8 hours.

Spicy Black Bean Sweet Potato Stew

Maria Shevlin, Sicklerville, NJ

Makes 3–4 servings

Prep. Time: 5 minutes ❧ *Cooking Time: 10 minutes* ❧ *Recommended Instant Pot size: 6-qt.*

2 tsp. olive oil

4 cloves garlic, minced

1 large onion, diced

8-oz. pkg. mushrooms, chopped

1¾ cups water

2 (14½-oz.) cans petite diced tomatoes

15½-oz. can black beans, rinsed and drained

4 sweet potatoes, peeled and cubed

1 vegetable bouillon cube

1 Tbsp. garlic powder

1 Tbsp. onion powder

1 Tbsp. parsley flakes

2 tsp. paprika

1 tsp. cumin

3 heaping Tbsp. Emeril's® Original Essence Seasoning Blend, *optional*

1. Set the Instant Pot to Sauté, then add the olive oil, garlic, and onion. Cook until just translucent.

2. Add the mushrooms and cook for 2 minutes longer.

3. Pour in the water and scrape up any bits from the bottom of the inner pot.

4. Add the remaining ingredients; stir.

5. Secure the lid and set the vent to sealing. Manually set the cook time for 8 minutes on high pressure.

6. When cook time is up, let the pressure release naturally for 5 minutes then manually release the remaining pressure.

Note:

If you don't want it spicy, you can omit the Essence.

Serving suggestion:

Serve with steamed rice, green onions, sour cream, or shredded sharp cheese.

Lentil-Tomato Stew

(Anonymous)

Makes 8 servings
Prep. Time: 10 minutes ❦ *Cooking Time: 4–12 hours* ❦ *Ideal slow-cooker size: 6-qt.*

3 cups water

28-oz. can low-sodium peeled Italian tomatoes, undrained

6-oz. can low-sodium tomato paste

½ cup dry red wine

¾ tsp. dried basil

¾ tsp. dried thyme

½ tsp. dried crushed red pepper

1 lb. dried lentils, rinsed and drained with stones removed

1 large onion, chopped

4 medium carrots, cut into ½-inch rounds

4 medium celery ribs, cut into ½-inch slices

3 cloves garlic, minced

1 tsp. salt

Chopped fresh basil or parsley

1. Combine 3 cups water, tomatoes with juice, tomato paste, wine, basil, thyme, and crushed red pepper in slow cooker.

2. Break up tomatoes with a wooden spoon; stir to blend them and the paste into the mixture.

3. Add lentils, onion, carrots, celery, and garlic.

4. Cover and cook on High 4 to 5 hours or on Low 10 to 12 hours.

5. Stir in salt.

6. Serve in bowls and sprinkle with chopped basil or parsley.

Pumpkin and Chickpea Stew

Andrea Maher, Dunedin, FL

Makes 6 servings
Prep. Time: 10 minutes ⚶ Cooking Time: 3–8 hours ⚶ Ideal slow-cooker size: 5- or 6-qt.

3 cups canned pumpkin puree

4 cups canned chickpeas, drained

3 cups sliced mushrooms

1½ cups gluten-free low-sodium vegetable broth

1½ cups plain nonfat Greek yogurt

Salt and pepper to taste

Red pepper and chili powder to taste, *optional*

1. Add all ingredients to slow cooker.

2. Cook on High 3–4 hours or Low 6–8.

Chilis

Chicken Chilis

Chicken Chili

Sharon Miller, Holmesville, OH

Makes 6 servings
Prep. Time: 15 minutes ❧ Cooking Time: 5–6 hours ❧ Ideal slow-cooker size: 4-qt.

2 lb. boneless, skinless chicken breasts, cubed

2 Tbsp. butter

2 (14-oz.) cans diced tomatoes, undrained

15-oz. can red kidney beans, rinsed and drained

1 cup diced onion

1 cup diced red bell pepper

1–2 Tbsp. chili powder, according to your taste preference

1 tsp. cumin

1 tsp. dried oregano

Salt and pepper to taste

1. In skillet on high heat, brown chicken cubes in butter until they have some browned edges. Place in greased slow cooker.

2. Pour one of the cans of tomatoes with its juice into skillet to get all the browned bits and butter. Scrape and pour into slow cooker.

3. Add rest of ingredients, including other can of tomatoes, to cooker.

4. Cook on Low for 5–6 hours.

Serving suggestion:

You can serve this chili with shredded cheddar cheese and sour cream.

White Chicken Chili

Judy Gascho, Woodburn, OR

Makes 6 servings

Prep. Time: 20 minutes ⚶ *Cooking Time: 30 minutes* ⚶ *Recommended Instant Pot size: 6-qt.*

2 Tbsp. cooking oil

1½–2 lb. boneless chicken breasts or thighs

1 medium onion, chopped

3 cloves garlic, minced

2 cups chicken broth

3 (15-oz.) cans great northern beans, undrained

15-oz. can white corn, drained

4½-oz. can chopped green chilies, undrained

1 tsp. cumin

½ tsp. ground oregano

1 cup sour cream

1½ cups grated cheddar or Mexican blend cheese

1. Set Instant Pot to Sauté and allow the inner pot to get hot.

2. Add oil and chicken. Brown chicken on both sides.

3. Add onion, garlic, chicken broth, undrained beans, drained corn, undrained green chilies, cumin, and oregano.

4. Place lid on and close valve to sealing.

5. Set to Bean/Chili for 30 minutes.

6. Let pressure release naturally for 15 minutes before carefully releasing any remaining steam.

7. Remove chicken and shred.

8. Put chicken, sour cream, and cheese in the inner pot. Stir until cheese is melted.

Serving suggestion:

Serve with chopped cilantro and additional cheese.

White Bean and Chicken Chili

SLOW COOKER

Hope Comerford, Clinton Township, MI

Makes 6–8 servings
Prep. Time: 15 minutes ❧ Cooking Time: 8–10 hours ❧ Ideal slow-cooker size: 5-qt.

2 lb. boneless, skinless chicken, cut into bite-sized chunks

½ cup dry navy beans, soaked overnight, rinsed and drained

½ cup dry great northern beans, soaked overnight, rinsed and drained

½ cup chopped carrots

1½ cups chopped onion

14½-oz. can petite diced tomatoes

10-oz. can diced tomatoes with lime juice and cilantro

5 cloves garlic, minced

6-oz. can tomato paste

1 Tbsp. cumin

1 Tbsp. chili powder

1 tsp. salt

¼ tsp. pepper

8 tsp. Better Than Bouillon® chicken base

8 cups water

1. Place all ingredients into the crock and stir to mix well.

2. Cover and cook on Low for 8–10 hours.

Southwestern Chili

SLOW COOKER

Colleen Heatwole, Burton, MI

Makes 12 servings
Prep. Time: 30 minutes & Cooking Time: 6–8 hours & Ideal slow-cooker size: 6- or 7-qt.

32-oz. can whole tomatoes

15-oz. jar salsa

15-oz. can low-sodium chicken broth

1 cup barley

3 cups water

1 tsp. chili powder

1 tsp. ground cumin

15-oz. can black beans

15-oz. can whole kernel corn

3 cups chopped cooked chicken

1 cup low-fat shredded cheddar cheese, *optional*

Low-fat sour cream, *optional*

1. Combine all ingredients in slow cooker except for cheese and sour cream.

2. Cover and cook on Low for 6–8 hours.

3. Serve with cheese and sour cream on each bowl, if desired.

Chicken Barley Chili

Colleen Heatwole, Burton, MI

Makes 10 servings
Prep. Time: 20 minutes   ♣   Cooking Time: 6–8 hours   ♣   Ideal slow-cooker size: 6-qt.

2 (14½-oz.) cans diced tomatoes

16-oz. jar salsa

1 cup quick-cooking barley, uncooked

3 cups water

1¾ cups chicken stock

15½-oz. can black beans, rinsed and drained

3 cups cubed cooked chicken or turkey

15¼-oz. can whole-kernel corn, undrained

1–3 tsp. chili powder, depending on how hot you like your chili

1 tsp. cumin

1 tsp. salt

⅛ tsp. pepper

1. Combine all ingredients in slow cooker.

2. Cover. Cook on Low 6–8 hours, or until barley is tender.

Serving suggestion:

Serve in individual soup bowls topped with sour cream and shredded cheese.

Turkey Chilis

Turkey Chili

Reita F. Yoder, Carlsbad, NM

Makes 8 servings
Prep. Time: 20 minutes ❧ Cook Time: 5 minutes ❧ Recommended Instant Pot size: 6-qt.

Olive oil or nonstick cooking spray

2 lb. ground turkey

1 small onion, chopped

1 clove garlic, minced

16-oz. can low-sodium pinto or kidney beans

2 cups chopped fresh tomatoes

2 cups no-salt-added tomato sauce

16-oz. can Ro-Tel® Diced Tomatoes and Green Chilies

1-oz. pkg. low-sodium chili seasoning

1. Turn the Instant Pot to Sauté and add a touch of olive oil or cooking spray to the inner pot. Crumble the ground turkey in the inner pot and brown on the Sauté setting until cooked. Add the onion and garlic and sauté an additional 5 minutes, stirring constantly.

2. Add remaining ingredients to inner pot and mix well.

3. Secure the lid and make sure the vent is set to sealing. Cook on Manual for 5 minutes.

4. When the cook time is over, let the pressure release naturally for 10 minutes, then manually release the rest.

White and Green Chili

Hope Comerford, Clinton Township, MI

Makes 6 servings
Prep. Time: 20 minutes ⚬ Cooking Time: 7–8 hours ⚬ Ideal slow-cooker size: 4-qt.

1 lb. lean ground turkey, browned

1 cup chopped onion

2 (15-oz.) cans great northern beans, rinsed and drained

16-oz. jar salsa verde (green salsa)

2 cups chicken broth

4-oz. can green chilies

1½ tsp. ground cumin

1 tsp. sea salt

¼ tsp. black pepper

2 Tbsp. chopped fresh cilantro

⅓ cup nonfat plain Greek yogurt, *optional*

1. Place all ingredients in crock except cilantro and Greek yogurt. Stir.

2. Cover and cook on Low for 7–8 hours. Stir in cilantro. Serve each bowl of chili with a dollop of the Greek yogurt, if using.

Serving suggestion:

Garnish with diced jalapeño peppers.

Black-Eyed Pea Chili

Lena Mae Janes, Lane, KS

Makes 10 servings

Prep. Time: 20–30 minutes ⚓ *Cooking Time: 2 hours* ⚓ *Ideal slow-cooker size: 5- or 6-qt.*

¾ lb. loose turkey sausage

1 medium onion, chopped

½ cup chopped celery

4 (15-oz.) cans black-eyed peas, undrained

14-oz. can low-sodium diced tomatoes, undrained

10-oz. can low-sodium diced tomatoes with green chilies, undrained

2 Tbsp. chili powder

1. Cook sausage in skillet until no longer pink, stirring frequently. Drain sausage on paper towel.

2. Add onion and celery to skillet. Cook until translucent, stirring frequently.

3. Place peas, tomatoes, tomatoes with green chilies, cooked onions and celery, sausage, and chili powder in slow cooker. Stir well.

4. Cover. Cook on High until all ingredients are hot, about an hour. Then turn cooker to Low and cook 1 more hour.

Pumpkin Black-Bean Turkey Chili

Rhoda Atzeff, Harrisburg, PA

Makes 10–12 servings

Prep. Time: 20 minutes ⚬ Cooking Time: 7–8 hours ⚬ Ideal slow-cooker size: 5-qt.

1 cup chopped onions

1 cup chopped yellow bell peppers

3 cloves garlic, minced

2 Tbsp. oil

1½ tsp. dried oregano

1½–2 tsp. ground cumin

2 tsp. chili powder

2 (15-oz.) cans black beans, rinsed and drained

2½ cups chopped cooked turkey

16-oz. can pumpkin

14½-oz. can diced tomatoes

3 cups chicken broth

1. Sauté onions, peppers, and garlic in oil in skillet for 8 minutes, or until soft.

2. Stir in oregano, cumin, and chili powder. Cook 1 minute. Transfer to slow cooker.

3. Stir in remaining ingredients.

4. Cover. Cook on Low 7–8 hours.

Serving suggestion:

Top with roasted pumpkin seeds.

Beef Chilis

Steak Chili

Jenny R. Unternahrer, Wayland, IA

Makes 4 servings

Prep. Time: 20–25 minutes ♣ *Cooking Time: 6–8 hours* ♣ *Ideal slow-cooker size: 3½-qt.*

16-oz. can kidney beans, drained

14½-oz. can low-sodium diced tomatoes

1 lb. lean top round steak, trimmed of fat and cubed

½ medium-sized onion, diced

⅓ green bell pepper, diced

1 clove garlic, minced

½ Tbsp. chili powder

¼ tsp. black pepper

½ tsp. salt

15-oz. can low-sodium tomato sauce

Several drops Tabasco® sauce, *optional*

1. Combine all ingredients in slow cooker. Stir.

2. Cover. Cook on Low 6–8 hours, or until meat is tender but not dry.

Carl's Steak Chili

(Anonymous)

Makes 4 servings

Prep. Time: 10 minutes ❧ *Cooking Time: 8 hours* ❧ *Ideal slow-cooker size: 3-qt.*

16-oz. can kidney beans, drained

14½-oz. can diced tomatoes

1 lb. lean top round steak, trimmed of fat and cubed

½ medium onion, diced

⅓ green bell pepper, diced

1 clove garlic, minced

½ Tbsp. chili powder

¼ tsp. black pepper

½ tsp. salt

15-oz. can low-sodium tomato sauce

Several drops of hot sauce, *optional*

Garnish:

Sour Cream

Shredded cheddar cheese

1. Combine all ingredients except garnishes in slow cooker. Stir. Cover and cook on Low 8 hours. Garnish with sour cream and cheddar cheese, if desired.

Our Favorite Chili

Ruth Shank, Gridley, IL

Makes 10–12 servings
Prep. Time: 20 minutes ⚶ *Cooking Time: 4–10 hours* ⚶ *Ideal slow-cooker size: 5-qt.*

1½ lb. extra-lean ground beef
¼ cup chopped onions
1 stalk celery, chopped
Extra-virgin olive oil, *optional*
29-oz. can stewed tomatoes
2 (15½-oz.) cans red kidney beans, rinsed and drained
2 (16-oz.) cans chili beans, undrained
½ cup ketchup
1½ tsp. lemon juice
2 tsp. vinegar
1 tsp. brown sugar
1½ tsp. kosher salt
1 tsp. Worcestershire sauce
½ tsp. garlic powder
½ tsp. dry mustard powder
1 Tbsp. chili powder
2 (6-oz.) cans tomato paste

1. Brown ground beef, onions, and celery in oil (if using) in skillet. Stir frequently to break up clumps of meat. When meat is no longer pink, drain off drippings.

2. Place meat and vegetables in slow cooker. Add all remaining ingredients. Mix well.

3. Cover. Cook on Low 8–10 hours or on High 4–5 hours.

Beer Chili

SLOW
COOKER

Hope Comerford, Clinton Township, MI

Makes 4–6 servings

Prep. Time: 20 minutes & Cooking Time: 7–8 hours & Ideal slow-cooker size: 5-qt.

½ lb. ground beef, browned

15¼-oz. can black beans, rinsed and drained

14½-oz. can diced tomatoes with green chilies

4-oz. can tomato sauce

12 oz. beer

1 large onion, chopped

1 beef bouillon cube

1 Tbsp. garlic powder

1 tsp. cumin

1 tsp. chili powder

1. Place all of the ingredients into the crock and stir.

2. Cover and cook on Low for 7–8 hours.

Serving suggestion:

Serve with corn muffins or crackers.

Tip:

If you like a more hearty chili, add more ground beef. For more spice, increase the cumin, or add a 4-oz. can diced green chilies.

Chipotle Beef Chili

Karen Ceneviva, Seymour, CT

Makes 8 servings
Prep. Time: 10–15 minutes ❧ *Cooking Time: 4–9 hours* ❧ *Ideal slow-cooker size: 3½-qt.*

16-oz. jar chunky chipotle salsa
1 cup water
2 tsp. chili powder
1 tsp. salt
1 large onion, chopped
2 lb. stewing beef, cut into ½-inch pieces
19-oz. can red kidney beans, rinsed and drained

1. Stir all ingredients together in slow cooker.

2. Cover. Cook on High 4–5 hours or on Low 8–9 hours, until beef is fork-tender.

Brown-Sugar Chili

SLOW COOKER

Alma Weaver, Ephrata, PA

Makes 8 servings

Prep. Time: 20 minutes   Cooking Time: 2 hours   Ideal slow-cooker size: 3½-qt.

1 lb. extra-lean ground beef
1 medium-sized onion, chopped
½ cup brown sugar
2 Tbsp. prepared mustard
2 (14-oz.) cans kidney beans, drained
1 pint low-sodium tomato juice
½ tsp. salt
¼ tsp. black pepper
1 tsp. chili powder

1. Brown lean ground beef and onion in nonstick skillet over medium heat. Stir brown sugar and mustard into meat.

2. Combine all ingredients in slow cooker.

3. Cover. Cook on High 2 hours. If it's convenient, stir several times during cooking.

Bison Chili

Willard E. Roth, Elkhart, IN

Makes 12 servings
Prep. Time: 20 minutes ❧ Cooking Time: 3–5 hours ❧ Ideal slow-cooker size: 7-qt.

1½ lb. ground bison

1 Tbsp. olive oil

1 tsp. ground cumin

1 Tbsp. chili powder

1 tsp. powdered garlic

1½ cups chopped onion

1 cup port, *divided*

4 (15-oz.) cans red kidney beans, *divided*

3 (15-oz.) cans diced tomatoes

⅓ cup dark brown sugar

4 (1-oz.) squares unsweetened baking chocolate (100% cacao)

1. In skillet, brown bison in oil with cumin, chili powder, garlic, onion, and ½ cup port for 15 minutes. Stir frequently, breaking up the meat into small chunks.

2. Spray slow cooker with cooking spray. Turn on High. Put in 3 cans of beans with liquid. Add meat mixture.

3. Stir in tomatoes and brown sugar.

4. In same skillet, melt baking chocolate, watching carefully so it doesn't burn.

5. Stir in remaining can of beans and liquid. Add to slow-cooker mixture.

6. Over medium heat, stir in remaining port, stirring up browned bits from skillet with a wooden spoon. When they're all loosened, add to slow cooker.

7. Cook on High for 3 hours, or Low for 5 hours.

Variation:

You can substitute ground beef (or venison) for the bison and have a wonderfully tasty dish!

Meatless Chilis

Garden Chili

Stacy Schmucker Stoltzfus, Enola, PA

Makes 10 servings

Prep. Time: 45 minutes   ♣   Cooking Time: 6–8 hours   ♣   Ideal slow-cooker size: 3½- or 4-qt.

¾ lb. onions, chopped

1 tsp. minced garlic

1 Tbsp. olive oil

¾ cup chopped celery

1 large carrot, peeled and thinly sliced

1 large green bell pepper, chopped

1 small zucchini, sliced

¼ lb. fresh mushrooms, sliced

1¼ cups water

14-oz. can kidney beans, rinsed and drained

14-oz. can low-sodium diced tomatoes with juice

1 tsp. lemon juice

⅛ tsp. dried oregano

1 tsp. ground cumin

1 tsp. chili powder

1 tsp. salt

1 tsp. black pepper

1. Sauté onions and garlic in olive oil in large skillet over medium heat until tender.

2. Add remaining fresh veggies. Sauté 2–3 minutes. Transfer to slow cooker.

3. Add remaining ingredients.

4. Cover. Cook on Low 6–8 hours.

Serving suggestion:
This is good served over rice.

Summer Chili

Hope Comerford, Clinton Township, MI

Makes 6 servings
Prep. Time: 15 minutes & Cooking Time: 3½–4 hours & Ideal slow-cooker size: 3-qt.

14.5-oz. can zucchini with Italian-style tomato sauce

14.5-oz. can diced tomatoes

15-oz. can tomato sauce

14-oz. can petite diced tomatoes with green chilies

15½-oz. can chili beans

15¼-oz. can black beans, rinsed and drained

1 medium onion, roughly chopped

3 small yellow squash, halved, quartered, and chopped

3 Tbsp. garlic powder

2 Tbsp. onion powder

1 tsp. salt

⅛ tsp. pepper

2 cups water

1. Place all ingredients into crock and stir.

2. Cover and cook on Low for 3½–4 hours.

Vegetarian Chili with Corn

SLOW COOKER

Jennifer Dzialowski, Brunton, MI

Makes 8–10 servings
Prep. Time: 20 minutes & *Cooking Time: 2–5 hours* & *Ideal slow-cooker size: 6-qt.*

2 (15-oz.) cans diced tomatoes, undrained

2 (15-oz.) cans kidney beans, drained

15-oz. can garbanzo beans, drained

15-oz. can corn, drained

1 bell pepper, chopped

½ cup, or more, chopped onions

6 cups low-sodium tomato juice

2 Tbsp. minced garlic

½ tsp. ground cumin

½ tsp. dried oregano

¼–½ tsp. black pepper, according to taste

1–3 tsp. chili powder, according to your taste preference

1 cup Textured Vegetable Protein (TVP)

1. Place tomatoes, kidney beans, garbanzo beans, corn, bell pepper, and onions in slow cooker.

2. Add tomato juice, garlic, cumin, oregano, black pepper, and chili powder. Top with Textured Vegetable Protein.

3. Cover. Cook on Low 4–5 hours or on High 2 hours.

Black Bean Chili

Kenda Autumn, San Francisco, CA

Makes 6–8 servings
Prep. Time: 15 minutes ❧ Cooking Time: 8 hours ❧ Ideal slow-cooker size: 5-qt.

1 Tbsp. olive oil

1 medium onion, chopped

1 tsp. ground cumin

1 tsp. ground coriander

1 Tbsp. chili powder

1 tsp. garam masala

16-oz. can black beans, rinsed and drained

14-oz. can diced tomatoes

1 sweet potato, cubed

2 cups cubed butternut squash

1 cup corn

1. Heat oil in saucepan. Brown onion with cumin, coriander, chili powder, and garam masala.

2. Transfer to slow cooker.

3. Add beans, tomatoes, sweet potato, butternut squash, and corn.

4. Cook on Low 8 hours.

Tip:

Use this recipe as a starting point for chili. I add other vegetables in step 3 that I have on hand, such as red bell pepper and mushrooms.

Chowders

Creamy Potato Chowder

Emily Fox, Bernville, PA

Makes 8 servings
Prep. Time: 15 minutes   ☘   Cooking Time: 8–10 hours   ☘   Ideal slow-cooker size: 5-qt.

8 cups diced potatoes

5½ cups chicken broth

10½-oz. can cream of chicken soup

⅓ cup chopped onion

¼ tsp. pepper

8 oz. cream cheese, cubed

½ lb. bacon, cooked and crumbled
minced chives

1. Combine the first five ingredients in the crock.

2. Cover and cook on Low 8–10 hours.

3. Add cream cheese; stir until blended. Garnish with bacon and chives.

Curried Chicken Chowder

(Anonymous)

Makes 6–8 servings
Prep. Time: 25 minutes ❧ Cooking Time: scan 6½–8½ hours ❧ Ideal slow-cooker size: 4-qt.

2 chicken leg quarters, skinned

1 onion, chopped

1 cup chopped celery, leaves included

1 medium potato, diced

3 carrots, sliced

1 cup frozen green beans

1½ tsp. salt

1 Tbsp. curry powder, *divided*

1 bay leaf

5 cups water

1 apple, peeled and diced

3 Tbsp. all-purpose flour

⅓ cup half-and-half, at room temperature

Garnish:

Chopped fresh parsley

1. Place chicken in slow cooker. Add chopped onion, celery, potato, carrots, green beans, salt, 1½ tsp. curry powder, and bay leaf. Pour 5 cups water over vegetables.

2. Cover and cook on Low 6–8 hours.

3. Remove chicken. Add diced apple and remaining 1½ tsp. curry powder.

4. Remove chicken from bones and return meat to slow cooker.

5. Whisk together flour and half-and-half in a small bowl until completely smooth. Whisk into hot soup. Cover and cook on Low 25 to 30 minutes more, stirring once or twice, until mixture is thick and apple is softened. Remove bay leaf before serving. Garnish with parsley, if desired.

Turkey Green Chili Chowder

Colleen Konetzni, Rio Rancho, NM

Makes 12 servings

Prep. Time: 45 minutes   ❧   *Cooking Time: 6 hours*   ❧   *Ideal slow-cooker size: 6-qt.*

1 cup chopped celery

1 cup chopped onion

1 ½ Tbsp. butter

3 cups chopped cooked turkey

4 cups low-sodium, fat-free turkey, or chicken, broth

4 potatoes, peeled or unpeeled, and cubed

½ cup chopped green chilies

½ cup cubed cheese, your choice

2 cans creamed corn

2 cups milk

1. In a skillet, sauté celery and onion in butter until vegetables soften and begin to brown.

2. Place sautéed vegetables, turkey, broth, potatoes, chilies, cheese, corn, and milk in slow cooker.

3. Cover. Cook on Low 6 hours, or until potatoes are soft.

4. If you wish, mash the chowder a few times with a potato masher to make it thicker.

5. Turn slow cooker to Low until time to serve.

Sausage and Kale Chowder

Beverly Hummel, Fleetwood, PA

Makes 6 servings

Prep. Time: 20 minutes ⚬ Cooking Time: 5 hours ⚬ Ideal slow-cooker size: 4- to 5-qt.

1 lb. bulk sausage
1 cup chopped onion
6 small red potatoes, chopped
1 cup thinly sliced kale, ribs removed
6 cups chicken broth
1 cup milk, at room temperature
Salt and pepper to taste

1. Brown sausage. Drain off grease. Transfer sausage to slow cooker.

2. Add onion, potatoes, kale, and broth.

3. Cook on High for 4 hours, until potatoes and kale are soft.

4. Add milk and cook on Low for 1 hour. Season to taste with salt and pepper.

Serving suggestion:

Italian bread and salad make a great accompaniment to this chowder.

Tip:

If you prefer a thicker soup, add 2 Tbsp. cornstarch to milk in Step 4 before adding to cooker. Stir several times in the last hour as chowder thickens.

Kale Chowder

Collen Heatwole, Burton, MI

Makes 8 servings

Prep. Time: 30 minutes ⚜ Cooking Time: 6 hours ⚜ Ideal slow-cooker size: 6-qt.

8 cups chicken broth

1 bunch of kale, cleaned, stems removed, and chopped

2 lb. potatoes, peeled and diced

4 cloves garlic, minced

1 onion, diced

1 lb. cooked ham

½ tsp. pepper, or to taste

1. Combine all ingredients in slow cooker.

2. Cover and cook on Low 6 hours, or until vegetables are tender.

Shrimp Chowder

Joanne Good, Wheaton, IL

Makes 12 servings
Prep. Time: 25 minutes ☙ Cooking Time: 7 hours ☙ Ideal slow-cooker size: 4-quart

1 medium onion, chopped

5 medium russet potatoes, peeled and cubed

1½ cups diced, pre-cooked ham

4–6 cups water

Salt and pepper, to taste

2 lb. shrimp, peeled, deveined, and cooked

Chowder Option:

4 Tbsp. flour

1 cup heavy (whipping) cream

1. Place chopped onion in microwave-safe bowl and cook in microwave for 2 minutes on High.

2. Place onion, cubed potatoes, diced ham, and 4 cups water in slow cooker. (If you're making the chowder option, whisk 4 Tbsp. flour into the 4 cups water in bowl before adding to slow cooker.)

3. Cover and cook on Low for 7 hours, or until potatoes are softened. If soup base is thicker than you like, add up to 2 cups more water.

4. About 15–20 minutes before serving, turn heat to High and add shrimp. If making chowder, also add heavy cream. Cook until shrimp are hot, about 15 minutes.

Creamy Salmon Chowder

Diane Shetler, Hyde Park, MA

Makes 5 servings
Prep. Time: 15–20 minutes & Cooking Time: 3¾–8¼ hours & Ideal slow-cooker size: 3½-qt.

2 cups chicken broth

2 cups water

10-oz. pkg. frozen corn

1 cup chopped celery

½ cup chopped onions

¾ cup dry wheat berries

8-oz. pkg. cream cheese, cut Into cubes

16-oz. can salmon, drained, skin and bones removed, and fish coarsely flaked

1 Tbsp. dill weed

1. Combine chicken broth, water, corn, celery, onions, and wheat berries in slow cooker.

2. Cover. Cook on Low 6–8 hours or on High 3½–4 hours.

3. Turn cooker to High. Add cheese, stirring until melted.

4. Stir in salmon and dill.

5. Cover. Cook 10 minutes longer.

Manhattan Clam Chowder

Joyce Slaymaker, Strasburg, PA
Louise Stackhouse, Benton, PA

Makes 8 servings
Prep. Time: 15 minutes   ♣   *Cooking Time: 8–10 hours*   ♣   *Ideal slow-cooker size: 3½-qt.*

¼ lb. salt pork, or bacon, diced and fried

1 large onion, chopped

2 carrots, thinly sliced

3 ribs celery, sliced

1 Tbsp. dried parsley flakes

28-oz. can diced tomatoes

½ tsp. salt

2–3 (8-oz.) cans clams, with liquid

2 whole peppercorns

1 bay leaf

1½ tsp. dried crushed thyme

3 medium potatoes, cubed

1. Combine all ingredients in slow cooker.

2. Cover. Cook on Low 8–10 hours. Remove bay leaf before serving.

Oceanside Bisque

Jane Geigley, Lancaster, PA

Makes 8 servings

Prep. Time: 30 minutes   Cooking Time: 2½–3½ hours   Ideal slow-cooker size: 6-qt.

1 Tbsp. unsalted butter

1 Tbsp. canola oil

3 large shallots or 1 Vidalia onion, minced

5 cups chicken stock

2 cups heavy cream

1 Tbsp. kosher salt

½ tsp. freshly ground white pepper

1 lb. fresh or thawed lump crabmeat (picked over for shell fragments), or canned crabmeat

½ cup dry sherry

Garnish:

Fresh tarragon or flat-leaf parsley

1. In small saucepan, melt butter and oil over medium heat.

2. Add shallots and sauté until translucent (about 2–3 minutes).

3. Pour into slow cooker.

4. Add stock and cream.

5. Season with salt and pepper.

6. Cook on High for ½ hour.

7. Add crabmeat and sherry.

8. Stir.

9. Cook for another 2–3 hours.

10. Ladle into bowls and garnish with tarragon or parsley.

Serving suggestion:

Serve with oyster crackers and cubed cheese. This is also delicious with fresh chopped parsley on top and a sprinkle of turmeric or paprika.

Potato and Corn Chowder

Janie Steele, Moore, OK

Makes 4–6 servings

Prep. Time: 10 minutes ⚬ *Cooking Time: 10 minutes* ⚬ *Recommended Instant Pot size: 6-qt.*

3 Tbsp. butter

¼ cup diced onion

6 medium red potatoes, diced

4 ears corn, or frozen or canned equal to 2 cups

3 cups vegetable broth or water

2 tsp. cornstarch

3 cups half-and-half

Grated cheddar cheese, *optional*

1. Place the butter in the inner pot of the Instant Pot. Press the Sauté function and let the butter melt.

2. Sauté the onion in the butter until translucent.

3. Add the potatoes, corn, and 3 cups broth or water to the Inner Pot.

4. Secure the lid and set vent to sealing, then cook on Manual, high pressure, for 10 minutes.

5. Let the pressure release naturally, then remove lid.

6. Mix cornstarch in small amount of water and mix into soup to thicken.

7. With Instant Pot on Sauté, add the half-and-half slowly while stirring.

8. Serve with cheddar cheese on top, if desired.

Corn Chowder

Janie Steele, Moore, OK

Makes 7 servings
Prep. Time: 30–35 minutes ⚬ Cooking Time: 5¼–6½ hours ⚬ Ideal slow-cooker size: 3½- or 4-qt.

4 large ears of corn, kernels cut off cob,
or 1-lb. bag frozen whole-kernel corn,
thawed

1 large onion, chopped

1 celery rib, chopped

1 Tbsp. butter

1½ cups potatoes, cubed

1 cup water

2 tsp. chicken bouillon granules

½ tsp. salt

¼ tsp. dried thyme

¼ tsp. pepper

6 Tbsp. flour

3 cups milk

1. Combine all ingredients in slow cooker except flour and milk.

2. Cook on Low 5–6 hours, or until potatoes are tender.

3. Mix flour and milk until smooth. Stir into corn chowder slowly until thickened. Cook 15–30 minutes more.

Stocks

Chicken Stock

Stacy Schmucker Stoltzfus, Enola, PA

Makes 3+ qt.
Prep. Time: 15 minutes ❧ *Cooking Time: 4–6 hours* ❧ *Ideal slow-cooker size: 6-qt.*

3 lb. chicken backs and necks, or whole chicken

3 qt. cold water

4 ribs celery, chopped coarsely

6 carrots, unpeeled, sliced thick

2 onions, peeled and quartered

8 peppercorns

1. Rinse chicken. Place in slow cooker. Add water and vegetables.

2. Cover. Cook on High 4–6 hours.

3. Remove chicken and vegetables from broth.

4. When broth has cooled slightly, place in refrigerator to cool completely. Remove fat and any foam when chilled.

5. The stock is ready for soup. Freeze it in 1-cup containers.

6. Use the cooked chicken and vegetables for soup or stews.

Veggie Stock

Char Hagner, Montague, MI

Makes 6 cups

Prep. Time: 15–20 minutes ❧ Cooking Time: 4–10 hours ❧ Ideal slow-cooker size: 4-qt.

2 tomatoes, chopped

2 onions, diced

4 carrots, diced

1 stalk celery, diced

1 potato, diced

6 cloves garlic

Dash salt

½ tsp. dried thyme

1 bay leaf

6 cups water

1. Combine tomatoes, onions, carrots, celery, potato, garlic, salt, thyme, bay leaf, and water.

2. Cover. Cook on Low 8–10 hours or on High 4–5 hours.

3. Strain stock through large sieve. Discard solids.

4. Freeze until needed (up to 3 months). Use for soups or stews.

Metric Equivalent Measurements

If you're accustomed to using metric measurements, I don't want you to be inconvenienced by the imperial measurements I use in this book.

Use this handy chart, too, to figure out the size of the slow cooker you'll need for each recipe.

Weight (Dry Ingredients)

1 oz		30 g
4 oz	¼ lb	120 g
8 oz	½ lb	240 g
12 oz	¾ lb	360 g
16 oz	1 lb	480 g
32 oz	2 lb	960 g

Slow-Cooker Sizes

1-quart	0.96 l
2-quart	1.92 l
3-quart	2.88 l
4-quart	3.84 l
5-quart	4.80 l
6-quart	5.76 l
7-quart	6.72 l
8-quart	7.68 l

Volume (Liquid Ingredients)

½ tsp.		2 ml
1 tsp.		5 ml
1 Tbsp.	½ fl oz	15 ml
2 Tbsp.	1 fl oz	30 ml
¼ cup	2 fl oz	60 ml
⅓ cup	3 fl oz	80 ml
½ cup	4 fl oz	120 ml
⅔ cup	5 fl oz	160 ml
¾ cup	6 fl oz	180 ml
1 cup	8 fl oz	240 ml
1 pt	16 fl oz	480 ml
1 qt	32 fl oz	960 ml

Length

¼ in	6 mm
½ in	13 mm
¾ in	19 mm
1 in	25 mm
6 in	15 cm
12 in	30 cm

Recipe and Ingredient Index

About the Author

Hope Comerford is a mom, wife, elementary music teacher, blogger, recipe developer, public speaker, Young Living Essential Oils essential oil enthusiast/educator, and published author. In 2013, she was diagnosed with a severe gluten intolerance and since then has spent many hours creating easy, practical, and delicious gluten-free recipes that can be enjoyed by both those who are affected by gluten and those who are not.

Growing up, Hope spent many hours in the kitchen with her Meme (grandmother) and her love for cooking grew from there. While working on her master's degree when her daughter was young, Hope turned to her slow cookers for some salvation and sanity. It was from there she began truly experimenting with recipes and quickly learned she had the ability to get a little more creative in the kitchen and develop her own recipes.

In 2010, Hope started her blog, *A Busy Mom's Slow Cooker Adventures*, to simply share the recipes she was making with her family and friends. She never imagined people all over the world would begin visiting her page and sharing her recipes with others as well. In 2013, Hope self-published her first cookbook, *Slow Cooker Recipes 10 Ingredients or Less and Gluten-Free*, and then later wrote *The Gluten-Free Slow Cooker*.

Hope became the new brand ambassador and author of Fix-It and Forget-It in mid-2016. Since then, she has brought her excitement and creativeness to the Fix-It and Forget-It brand. Through Fix-It and Forget-It, she has written *Fix-It and Forget-It Healthy Slow Cooker Cookbook*, *Fix-It and Forget-It Instant Pot Cookbook*, *Fix-It and Forget-It Plant-Based Comfort Foods Cookbook*, *Welcome Home Harvest Cookbook*, *Welcome Home Pies, Crisps, and Crumbles*, *Fix-It and Forget-It Instant Pot Light & Healthy Cookbook*, and many more.

Hope lives in the city of Clinton Township, Michigan, near Metro Detroit. She has been happily married to her husband and best friend, Justin, since 2008. Together they have two children, Ella and Gavin, who are her motivation, inspiration, and heart. In her spare time, Hope enjoys traveling, singing, cooking, reading books, working on wooden puzzles, spending time with friends and family, and relaxing.